GLOBALIZATION OF RESEARCH & DEVELOPMENT

GLOBALIZATION OF RESEARCH & DEVELOPMENT

FOREIGN RESEARCH AND DEVELOPMENT ACTIVITIES OF MNEs IN INDIA AND CHINA

SWAPAN KUMAR PATRA
&
MAMMO MUCHIE

AFRICA WORLD PRESS
TRENTON | LONDON | CAPE TOWN | NAIROBI | ADDIS ABABA | ASMARA | IBADAN | NEW DELHI

AFRICA WORLD PRESS
541 West Ingham Avenue | Suite B
Trenton, New Jersey 08638

Copyright © 2022 Swapan Kumar Patra & Mammo Muchie

All rights reserved. No part of this publication may be reproduced, stored in a retrieval system or transmitted in any form or by any means electronic, mechanical, photocopying, recording or otherwise without the prior written permission of the publisher.

Book & cover design: Lemlem Tadesse

Cataloging-in-Publication Data may be obtained from the Library of Congress.

ISBNs: 978-1-56902-772-1 (HB)
        978-1-56902-773-8 (PB)

Dedication

To all children to learn to build one community with unity, with values and practice in reality Ubuntu and humanity as one family.

TABLE OF CONTENT

LIST OF ILLUSTRATIONS xi
  List of Figures xi
  List of Tables xii
PREFACE xv
ACKNOWLEDGEMENT xvii
CHAPTER I. INTRODUCTION 1
  Trends in Internationalization of R&D 5
  Research Trends 6
  Subject areas 7
  Journals 8
  Country 9
  Objectives 13
  Organization of the Book 14
  Summary 15
CHAPTER II. THEORETICAL FRAMEWORK 17
  Introduction 17
  Role of MNEs in Globalization process 19
  Internationalization vs. Globalization 20
  Internationalization of R&D 24
  Evolution of Global R&D 26
  Global Research Trends 28
  Costs and Benefits of global R&D 31
  Motivation and Driving Forces 35
  Globalization of R&D from developing country's
    perspective 40

Foreign R&D and Capacity building................... 42
Innovation and Network................................... 44
R&D Networks... 45
Modes of Alliances.. 48
Summary.. 51
CHAPTER III. RESEARCH ON FOREIGN R&D IN
INDIA AND CHINA 53
Introduction... 53
Foreign R&D in India...................................... 54
Scholarly Research on foreign R&D in India... 55
Foreign R&D in China.................................... 59
Scholarly Research on foreign R&D in China... 61
Summary.. 67
CHAPTER IV. MOTIVATION OF FOREIGN R&D BY
FIRMS IN INDIA AND CHINA 69
Introduction... 69
Motivations to set up foreign R&D................. 71
Motivations to Set up R&D in India................ 73
Motivation of firms to set up R&D units in India –
selected cases... 74
Foreign R&D in China.................................... 77
Motivations to set up R&D in China............... 79
Motivation of firms to set up R&D units in China –
Selected cases... 81
General Expansion.. 84
Summary.. 84
CHAPTER V. FIRMS AND THEIR INNOVATION
POTENTIAL IN INDIA AND CHINA 87
Introduction... 87
R&D performance measurement of firms....... 89
Publication activities of firms......................... 91
Growth of publications 94
Patenting activities of firms............................ 95
Patent portfolio of firms 96
Innovation from India and China – Selected cases 99

Summary 102
CHAPTER VI. LINKAGES AND KNOWLEDGE
  SPILLOVER 105
  Introduction 105
  Multinational Firms' Embeddedness with the local
    Innovation System 108
  Social Network Analysis 109
  Collaboration of Firms in India and China 110
  Pharmaceutical firms' linkages in India 110
  Pharmaceutical firms' linkages in China 114
  ICT Firms' Linkages 117
  Collaboration of ICT firm's joint publication with
    various actors in India 118
  Patent collaboration networks in pharmaceutical
    industry 124
  Collaboration network in ICT industry 128
  Knowledge Spillover 131
CHAPTER VII. DISCUSSION AND CONCLUDING
  REMARKS 141
  Introduction 141
  Major Findings 143
  Policy recommendations 150
APPENDIX 157
  Appendix I Search string used to search scholarly
    publications of the respective firms 157
  Appendix II Search string used to search scholarly
    publications of the respective firm's publications from
    India 163
  Appendix III Search string used to search scholarly
    publications of the respective firms from China 171
  Appendix IV Search string used to search patents of the
    respective firms 180
BIBLIOGRAPHY 183
INDEX 219

LIST OF ILLUSTRATIONS

List of Figures

Figure 1 FDI Inflows and outflows from India and China in recent years 3
Figure 2. Growth of globalization of R&D literature 6
Figure 3 Subject areas of Globalization of R&D literature 7
Figure 4. Growth of literatue in ICT and Pharmaceuticle firms from India and China 94
Figure 5. Growth of patents of ICT and Pharmaceutical firms from India and China 99
Figure 6. Network map of pharmaceutical firms' co-authorship in India 112
Figure 7. Network map of pharmaceutical firms' co-authorship in China 115
Figure 8. Network map of ICT firms' co-authorship in India 118
Figure 9. Network map of ICT firms' co-authorship in China 120
Figure 10. Network map of pharmaceutical firms' patent network in India 125
Figure 11. Network map of pharmaceutical firms' patent network in China 126
Figure 12. Network map of ICT firms' patent network in India 129

Figure 13. Network map of ICT firms' patent network in China 130

List of Tables

Table 1. FDI inflows, by region and economy 2015–2020 (Millions of dollars) 2
Table 2. FDI outflows, by region and economy 2015–2020 (Millions of dollars) 3
Table 3 Top journals of publication of Globalization of R&D literature 8
Table 4. Country of publication of Globalization of R&D literature 9
Table 5. Major literature of interest in Internationalization R&D 28
Table 6. Scholarly research output of firms in ICT and Pharmaceutical sector 92
Table 7. Shows the patent portfolio of firms from India and China. 96
Table 8. Centrality measures of pharmaceutical firms' co-authorship in India 113
Table 9. Centrality measures of pharmaceutical firms' co-authorship in China 116
Table 10. Centrality measures of ICT firms' co-authorship in India 119
Table 11. Centrality measures of ICT firms' co-authorship in China 121
Table 12. Joint patents of firms from India and China 123
Table 13. Centrality measure of pharmaceutical firms' collaborative patents in India 126
Table 14. Centrality measure of pharmaceutical firms' collaborative patents in China 127
Table 15. Centrality measure of ICT firms' collaborative patents in India 129
Table 16. Centrality measure of ICT firms' collaborative patents in China 130

Table 17. Example of spin off firms from foreign R&D
   centres in India...135
Table 18. Examples of training programs by foreign firms
   in China...136
Table 19. Examples of training programs by foreign firms
   in India..137

PREFACE

Since last couple of decades, there is an increasing trend of MNEs Research and Development (R&D) in the offshore location. MNEs of developed countries of global North are accessing R&D capabilities to strengthen their home base from other developing countries in the global South. The present wave of globalization has shown main destination of these firms are in India and China. This phenomenon offers interesting research problems to analyze and raise research questions like what are the drivers of these firms to come to these countries. What kind of R&D these firms in these two host countries are conducting? How they are linked with the various actors of local innovation system? With these research questions, this book is a comparative exploratory study of the foreign R&D firms in India and China using secondary data, for example, publication and patent data to answer the research questions raised above. The study uses various bibliometric, scientometric and Social Network Analysis tools. The research also uses various newspaper reports and employed content analysis tools to extract motivation of firms to go offshore.

This book is based on 10 ICT firms and 10 Pharmaceutical industry form. The firms in pharmaceutical industry are as follows; AstraZeneca AB, Bristol Myers Squibb, Eli Lilly & Co., GlaxoSmithKline plc, Johnson & Johnson, Merck & Co., Inc., Novartis AG, Novo Nordisk A/S, Pfizer Inc. and Sanofi S.A. ICT industry firms are further categorized into three groups.

The 10 ICT industry firms are as follows: Communications Equipment industry firms (Cisco Systems, Inc., Hewlett Packard Enterprise Company, Motorola Solutions, Nokia Corporation and Telefonaktiebolaget LM Ericsson). The Software & Services industry firm are (International Business Machines Corporation, Microsoft Corporation). The Semiconductor equipment industry firms are (Intel Corporation, Qualcomm Technologies, Inc., Samsung Electronics Co Ltd and Texas Instruments Incorporated)

Scholarly publication data for analysis is extracted from Scopus data of Elsevier science. The patent data was extracted from the World Intellectual Property (WIPO) data from the Patent scope database.

The evidences show that firms are increasing their R&D activities in both these countries. However, there is still a lack of conclusive evidences that firms are doing significant R&D in these countries in India and China.

ACKNOWLEDGEMENT

Thanks to the DSI/NRF SARChi chair on Innovation Studies with Industrial Engineering Department, Faculty of Engineering and the Built Environment, Tshwane University of Technology for their support.

CHAPTER I. INTRODUCTION

The present wave of 'Economic globalization' includes the growing interdependence of locations and economic units across different countries and regions. With the globalization of production, international economics is changing rapidly. The unparalleled technological change in modern time and the increasing significance of Multinational Enterprises (MNEs) are perhaps the major reason of this present globalization process. MNEs are extending their business within very competitive and fast-moving market conditions. The MNEs often invests abroad in order to gain revenues and profits out of innovations embodied in the products or services developed at the home base of the firm. The MNEs sell these products in the global, regional or domestic markets. They gain competitive advantage by exploiting global economies of scale and by arbitraging imperfections in the world's capital, materials, and labor markets. They developed product and service designed and manufactured based on the world's most advanced technological expertise. MNEs are also very responsive to the product variations based on the local market condition (Katz, et al., 1996).

World Investment Report (WIR 2009) estimated that, there are about 82,000 MNEs worldwide, with 810,000 subsidiaries. These subsidiaries altogether employed about 77 million people in 2008 (UNCTAD, 2009). Due to their big size, both in terms of money and human resources, MNEs play major roles in the global economy. They are also the main actor of present-day globalization process. Foreign Direct Investment (FDI) is one of the main mechanisms through which MNEs acquire assets abroad or set up new wholly owned activities abroad. Beside FDI there are other mechanisms for example, trade, licensing, patenting technological and scientific collaborations by which MNEs form linkages with the entities in the foreign countries.

According to World Investment Report (WIR) of 2021, due to the COVID-19 pandemic there is major fall in foreign direct investment (FDI) in 2020. The global FDI flows fallen by 35 per cent to $1 trillion, from $1.5 trillion in 2019. WIR 2021 report further observed that the FDI flow was almost 20 per cent below the 2009 level after the global financial crisis. China receives about 149,342 million dollars of inflow and India receives about 64, 062 million dollars of inward FDI in the year 2020 (Table 1.1). Both India and China receive a major chunk of FDI inflows among the developing economics (UNCTAD, 2021).

Table 1. *FDI inflows, by region and economy 2015–2020 (Millions of dollars)*

Region/ Economy	FDI inflows					
	2015	2016	2017	2018	2019	2020
World	2032298	2065238	1647312	1436732	1530228	998891
Developed economies	1267808	1344533	894321	707649	748999	312170
Developing economies	730434	653885	702495	692480	723385	662562
Asia	514307	470818	505154	496473	515548	535324
China	135577	133711	136315	138305	141225	149342
India	44064	44481	39904	42156	50558	64062

(Source: UNCTAD, 2021)

INTRODUCTION

Table 2. FDI outflows, by region and economy 2015-2020 (Millions of dollars)

Region/ Economy	FDI outflows					
	2015	2016	2017	2018	2019	2020
World	1698209	1616138	1604697	870715	1220432	739872
Developed economies	1262783	1173389	1087409	430584	780489	347162
Developing economies	403323	417562	478816	402530	416620	387069
Asia	372364	397577	430469	392197	364290	388797
China	145667	196149	158290	143037	136905	132940
India	7572	5072	11141	11447	13144	11560

(Source: UNCTAD, 2021)

However, in term of FDI outflows China has invested about 132,940 million USD and India about 11,560 FDI in 2020 (Table 1.2). China is well ahead in terms of investment globally. It is evident from the Chinese activities in many countries globally. Figure 1.1 shows the trends of FDI inflows and outflows from these countries during the year 2015-2020. WIR 2021 have observed that Inflows in China has increased even during pandemic. It was increased, by 6 per cent, to $149 billion. In India the increasing investment was due to Merger and Acquisition (M&A) activities.

Figure 1 FDI Inflows and outflows from India and China in recent years

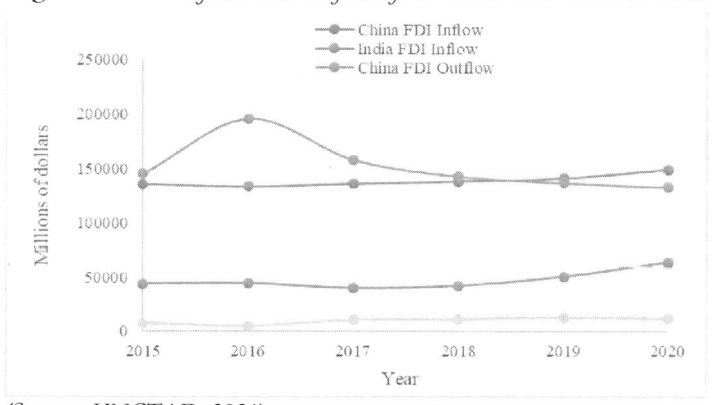

(Source: UNCTAD, 2021)

Although there is a major decline in the recent FDI in developing countries. The FDI projects are in the primary sectors and in many services, industries including, environment and renewable energies, information and communication technologies (ICT), health care and biotechnology. The major motives behind the growth of FDI are *market-seeking, resource-seeking* (human resource at low cost, raw materials, finance, venture capital), *stable investment environment* and to host *government effectiveness*. Regarding the internationalization of corporate functions, companies are not only investing in manufacturing, assembly, and distribution, but also in other administrative functions, and above all in even in critical R&D activities (UNCTAD, 2007).

R&D activities that were earlier regarded as the least preferred activity in internationalization process of MNEs are increasingly getting prominence. Companies consider to access high skilled and low-cost talent all over the globe. Big firms consider, R&D in the offshore to increase innovation capabilities to gain edge over their competitor. Companies adopt different means to implement their global sourcing strategies in R&D. The strategy includes, joint research, contract research, university collaboration, acquisition of patents and licenses, and finally setting up of R&D centers abroad. UNCTAD publication, "World Investment Prospect Survey 2007–2009." found that MNEs prefer South, East and South-East Asia as an investment opportunity. The main reasons behind this preference are; low-cost labor, new market, high skilled power available at low cost. These all factors provide huge growth potential and attractive location for firms to invest in these countries. Further, the firm's prefer Greenfield investments than Merger and Acquisition (M&A) as an entry mode in these economics (UNCTAD, 2007).

There are a number of different actors in globalization of Research and Development (R&D) and innovation. However, MNEs have the central role in globalization of innovation (Narula & Zanfei, 2005). Archibugi & Pietrobelli (2003) identified three different types of globalization process. These categories are *international exploitation of nationally produced technology; the global generation of innovation; global technological collaborations.* Big MNEs may generate innovations through all these three processes. According *to World Investment Report 2005* (WIR 2005), MNEs spent about half of global R&D expenditures, and about two thirds of business R&D expenditures (UNCTAD, 2005). This figure is even higher than many less developed countries' Gross Domestic Product (GDP). However, this investment concentrated in a few high-tech industries for example in Information Technology, automobile, pharmaceuticals and biotechnology industry (UNCTAD, 2005). The R&D spending in high technology sectors shows that the MNEs are not only the actor in the generation but also in diffusion of innovation. MNEs use different means through which innovation develops and diffuses across national borders.

Trends in Internationalization of R&D

Internationalization by MNEs is not a new development. A stream of literature exists in the internationalization of multinational firms. However, Internationalization of R&D was not a prominent gained focus by scholars until the early 1980's. Few early studies for example Ronstadt (1977) Behrman & Fischer (1980) studied US based MNCs and observed that R&D activities of MNEs. Various studies observed that there was and increasing trends of R&D abroad. The offshoring of R&D happened due to various push and pull factors. However, new trends emerged in late 80's when there was speedy increase in foreign-funded and foreign-performed R&D in most developed countries. *OECD Science and Technology Indicators Report* and the *United States National Science Board Science and Engineering Indicators* observed that in early 1990s, that there was an acceleration in the internationalization of industrial R&D (Niosi, 1999). By the end of 1990s; however, it had become an important research area. Scholarly journals also deal with the subject in depth. There are many scholarly journals specially dealt with the issue and come up with special issues like *IEEE Transactions on Engineering Management* 1996 Volume 43, Issue 1, and *Research Policy* 1999 Volume 28 Issue 2-3, *Journal of Technology Transfer* 2006 volume 33 to name a few.

Research Trends

A literature search on Scopus database of Elsevier Science conducted to study the research trend on the globalization of R&D. The Scopus is an indexing and abstracting database launched by the Elsevier Science in the year 2004 and now it covers about 25,100 titles from more than 5,000 international publishers (Scopus Content Coverage Guide 2020). With its wide coverage, this database is used to search the research trends on this topic globally. This research trend will give an insight on the literature publication growth, the subject wise distribution of the topic, the core journal where the articles are published and the institute and country from where the publications are coming from. Using the key words "Internationalization of R&D" OR "Globalization of R&D" OR "Globalization of Innovation" shows 2,939 articles during 1985-2020. The result shows that there was a sharp increase in scholarly literature since 1999. Today more than 150 scholarly articles published annually in peer-reviewed journals globally (Figure 1.2).

Figure 2. Growth of globalization of R&D literature

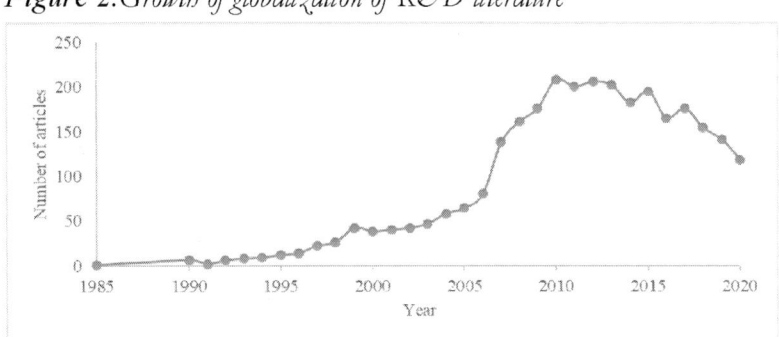

The new research trends in recent years proposed many theoretical frameworks and hypothesis. The earlier concept of internationalization R&D considered as a one-way process and contested as Globalization of R&D and Innovation, a global phenomenon of R&D. Some of the empirical evidences has suggested that MNE's foreign R&D laboratories today are not only confined to adaption of parent company's technology to host countries, but gradually developing as major innovations for the needs of global market.

Subject areas

Scopus database covers peer-reviewed literature globally in almost all branches of knowledge including science, technology, social sciences and arts & humanities (A&H). Scopus classifies the universe of knowledge into four broad subject clusters (life sciences, physical sciences, health sciences and social sciences & humanities). Further, subjects sub-divided into 27 major subject areas and more than 300 minor subject areas.

Figure 3 Subject areas of Globalization of R&D literature

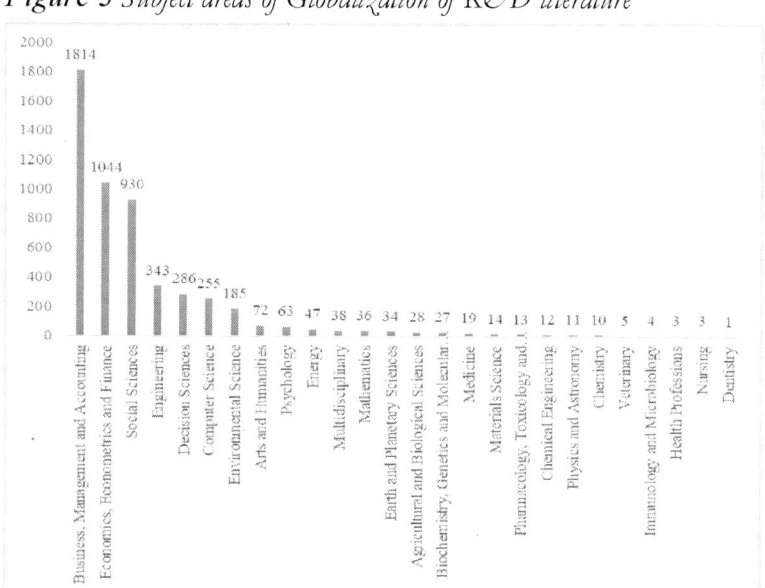

A further analysis of the 2,939 articles shows that most of the literature are in the subject areas of Business, Management and Accounting followed by Economics, Econometrics and Finance (Figure 1.3).

Journals

Journals are the major output indicators of any scholarly research. There are more than 25,100 journals indexed Scopus. It covers 12,464 journals in Social Sciences, 14,448 journals in Health sciences and 13,312 journals in Physical sciences and 7,295 journals in Life sciences. Hence, Scopus has wide coverage of journals in a wide variety of subjects as well as global publishers. The retrieved literature on this research shows that most of the research was published in the journal Research policy (Table 1.3). Among the total 2,939 articles from the retrieved records, the journal Research policy publish 114 articles (about 4 percent of the total articles).

Table 3 Top journals of publication of Globalization of R&D literature

Sl. NO	Name of the journal	Number of articles	Percentage of total articles
1.	Research Policy	114	3,88
2.	International Journal of Technology Management	51	1,74
3.	Journal Of International Business Studies	50	1,70
4.	Technological Forecasting and Social Change	46	1,57
5.	International Business Review	38	1,29
6.	Management International Review	34	1,16
7.	Journal Of International Management	33	1,12
8.	Regional Studies	29	0,99
9.	Science And Public Policy	27	0,92
10.	European Planning Studies	25	0,85
11.	Sustainability Switzerland	25	0,85
12.	Journal Of Technology Transfer	24	0,82

13.	R And D Management	24	0,82
14.	Journal Of World Business	23	0,78
15.	Science Technology and Society	23	0,78
16.	Industrial And Corporate Change	21	0,71
17.	Strategic Management Journal	21	0,71
18.	Technology Analysis and Strategic Management	21	0,71
19.	Asia Pacific Journal of Management	20	0,68

Country

The country wise analysis of articles shows that most of the articles were published from the United States. Among the total 2,939 articles, there were about 613 articles (about 21 percent) articles published from the US followed by United Kingdom (16 percent). From China there are about 186 articles (4.12 percent), and about India 121 articles (4, 12 percent) are published from China and India affiliation. Therefore, it is evident from the table 1.4. That significant number of literatures on the topic is published from the developed part of the global north. The global south including India and China still lagging behind in terms of the publication on the topic.

Table 4. Country of publication of Globalization of R&D literature

Sl. Number	Country	Number of articles	Percentage of total articles
1.	United States	613	20,86
2.	United Kingdom	480	16,33
3.	Italy	218	7,42
4.	Germany	214	7,28
5.	China	186	6,33
6.	Netherlands	137	4,66
7.	Spain	134	4,56
8.	India	121	4,12
9.	Sweden	120	4,08
10.	Canada	117	3,98
11.	Denmark	117	3,98

12.	France	116	3,95
13.	Brazil	91	3,10
14.	Australia	78	2,65
15.	South Korea	76	2,59
16.	Switzerland	76	2,59
17.	Japan	74	2,52
18.	Taiwan	70	2,38
19.	Austria	69	2,35
20.	Belgium	61	2,08

Therefore, it is evident from the scientometric analysis of published literature that, since the late 1990s the world witnessed a period of accelerated R&D globalization. Firms have realized that knowledge is the most important and independent source of competitiveness, innovation, and growth. With the increasing global competition, MNEs are internationalizing their knowledge-intensive corporate functions from dispersed global learning centers. Although, MNEs usually keep their crucial R&D activities close to their home base, their science, technology, and innovation processes are becoming more open and spread both geographically (globally) and functionally (along the global value chain) (Gammeltoft, 2005). In the process of global expansion, MNEs set up their R&D centre to satisfy the local customers' need. Further, with the increasing local consumers and markets become more demanding, MNEs generally try to shift their R&D units beyond a simple technology transfer unit (TTU) (Ronstadt, 1977).

Moreover, foreign R&D by MNE was limited between the developed countries only. More specifically, foreign R&D by MNEs was particularly limited into the Triads (US, European Union and Japan). Now, the traditional course of Internationalization of R&D is no longer limited to 'triad'. Now the R&D investment is going more towards developing countries. Firms are increasingly investing in developing countries particularly in Asian countries. *"World Investment Report 2005: Transnational Corporations and the Internationalization of*

INTRODUCTION

R&D" (UNCTAD, 2005) reported that developing countries are now no longer the only capital and technology exporters. The countries from the global south are emerging as 'knowledge hub'. MNEs are now looking at the developing world particularly the two new and emerging countries i.e., India and China as sources of not only cheap labor, but also of growth, skills and even new technologies. To exploit knowledge and resources from these two countries new organizational practices are being evolved by the enterprises, to enhance their efficiency, to access expanding pools of scientists and engineers, and to meet the demands of increasingly sophisticated markets. So, the latest trend is that both India and China are increasingly receiving FDI in more knowledge-intensive activities (UNCTAD, 2005).

World Investment Report (WIR) 2005 study shows that the degree of internationalization of R&D is rising. The previous notions of R&D - the least internationalize activity of MNEs and the concept that they are mainly doing R&D for the local adaptations are changing. For example; Intel Corporation's Hyderabad facility, employs about 400 engineers planning to hire more than 1000 employees to develop critical global products and technologies (ET Bureau, 2019). *Motorola*'s R&D centers in China has about 1,300(Motorola opens new R&D Centre 2006), *GE's John F Welch Technology Cen*tre located in various Indian cities. John F. Welch technology center is the largest facilities for GE's research outside the US. It employs more than 4,000 engineers and scientists. Microsoft have two R&D centers in India. The first one established in January 2005 in Bengaluru known as the Microsoft Research India, (MSR India). The second one Microsoft India (R&D) Pvt. Ltd established in Hyderabad in 1998. Now these two centers are Microsoft's largest R&D centers outside its headquarters in Redmond (Leslie D'Monte, 2017). As seen from the above examples, and from other examples, it is evident that R&D by MNEs in foreign location is no longer a mere adaptation to local market condition (UNCTAD, 2005).

Both the countries are the major receiver of FDI in R&D. However, Chinese case is more focused and highlighted than India in the international scenario (Patra 2014). A number of studies on focusing R&D in China is being conducted by various national and international agencies in different span of time. *OECD Reviews of Innovation Policy CHINA Synthesis Report, 2007, OECD Review of Innovation Policy: China* full report 2008, UNCTAD Report on *Globalization of R&D and Developing Countries* published in 2005, *Coming of Age: Multinational Companies in China* by Economic Intelligence Unit in 2004 are to name a few. Beside these, many scholarly journals, for example *Asia pacific Business Review* Volume 13 July 2007, *Journal of Technology Transfer* Volume 32, 2007, *R&D Management* volume 34 no 4 2004, *International Journal of Technology and Globalization* Volume 3 Number 4, 2007 *International Journal of Technology Management*, Vol. 51, Nos. 2/3/4, 2010, have come up with special issues. These special issues dealt with the various aspects of foreign R&D by MNEs and their experience in doing business in China (Patra & Krishna, 2015).

The theories of globalization of R&D have derived from different perspectives. The research area encompasses, various branches of social science including economics; management. Some of the major works borrow heavily from economic theories of 'international operations of firms. Innovation studies are also contributing to this evolving debate and developing an analytical framework that can help explain the 'internationalization of R&D'. Almost all the research related to internationalization of corporate R&D has been carried out so far related to the industrialized developing countries particularly the inward or outward FDI in R&D in triads. There are very limited studies (Reddy, 1997; Reddy, 2000; Reddy 2011; Patra & Krishna, 2015; Krishna, Patra & Bhattacharya, 2012, Mrinalini, 2009, Mrinalini, & Wakdikar 2008) that have built the analytical framework for globalization of R&D in India. Although China is increasingly getting focus, there are no major studies except a few (on Internationalization of R&D in India. However, as highlighted above they do not yet provide a strong dominant theoretical framework. Keeping this limitation in consideration, the present study would be exploratory in nature. The important influential works on 'Globalization of R&D' would be used as markers. This will help in articulation and explanation of the empirical data that would be captured thorough the exploratory study. This study will essentially cover the various aspects of foreign R&D in India and China. The evolution of foreign R&D firms in India and China will be investigated. Empirical evidences will be used to determine whether they are opening new avenues of research, creating knowledge oriented global hub, creating proprietary knowledge, etc.

Objectives

The study will look into the foreign R&D firms in India and China in terms of their motivation, innovation potential (publication and patents) and linkages (examined though co-authored publication and joint patents) with different actors in the innovation system.

Some of the research questions that would address the above objective:

- What are the factors that have motivated the establishment of foreign R&D firms?
- How the R&D units of firms are doing in R&D in terms of selected case studies from various sources
- How they are doing in terms of publications and patents?
- How the R&D units of selected firms are interacting with various actors within the innovation system: government, university, Indian firms, market? What types of exchanges that take place among the various actors?
- How the firms are embedded in the research and innovation system.

Organization of the Book

The subject matter of this book has been organized in seven chapters.

Chapter 1 reviews the central issue of this book. This chapter deals with the foreign R&D multinationals encompassing the genesis of foreign R&D, new trends that have emerged in the literature. The chapter covers conceptual framework objectives and research questions that this study addresses.

Chapter 2 reviews the literature on internationalization and globalization of R&D. The various research works reviewed in details. Based on this review and the analytical frameworks the chapter identified, the research knowledge gap. The chapters follows analyses the various issues based on the analytical frameworks identified, and justification of this study is given.

Chapter 3 will analyze the broad overview of foreign R&D in India and China. This chapter traces the pattern and growth of foreign R&D in India and China. The chapter explores the general trends of the foreign R&D by firms in India and China from the secondary literature.

Chapter 4 will deal with motivation of foreign R&D activity by selected firms in ICT and pharmaceutical sectors. The motivations of firms are taken under broad heading of talent, market, global product development and general expansion and so on.

Chapter 5 summarizes the major findings of the study. It studies the R&D and Innovation activities by Foreign Firms by considering two major output indicators (patents and publications). The chapter is dwell upon deeper theoretical issues i.e., whether empirical data analysis enriches our understanding of foreign R&D in developing countries and their implications.

Chapter 6 analyzes the orientation, linkages and interactions of foreign R&D firms. This chapter covers interactions with different actors of the innovation system in terms of types of linkages taking place, whether these linkages has translated into tangible outcomes (say, joint research projects, new products/processes developed) etc. The crucial issue of knowledge spillover is also presented in this chapter.

Chapter 7 summarizes the 'key' findings of the study and their implications for further research. It also indicates their policy implications. The chapter also provides suggestions and scope for future studies.

Summary

In sum, Multinational Enterprises (MNEs) are the main driver of globalization. MNEs used to exploit their strong home-based technological capabilities abroad. Since the early 1980's there was an emerging trend of FDI in R&D in offshore locations. These phenomena renewed interest among the economists, policy and decision makers and so on in different level. It was observed by many scholars that MNEs not only exploit their home-based strength aboard but also, they exploit host country's strength to augment their S&T and knowledge. This phenomenon was observed among the MNEs originated from the 'triad'. They usually invest in and among the triad. However, the first decade of 21st century observed a new trend where the large MNEs increasingly investing in R&D in developing countries of east. The main destinations are in China and India. Theses phenomenon renewed interest among scholars with the inquiry that why these corporates are interested in doing R&D in these two countries. The issue is of concern for both host as well as host countries perspective. Although, a lot of literature available on the various issues of MNEs behavior among the developed countries. The literature on this recent phenomenon is lacking. The China has got more focus than India, perhaps due to its size and depth of R&D as it is covered by various media.

This book is a comparative analysis of selected firms R&D activities in India and China. The first chapter has given a brief overview of the phenomenon. The second chapter will cover the literature on globalization of R&D.

CHAPTER II. THEORETICAL FRAMEWORK

Introduction

Globalization is one of the most hotly debated topic in international economics since the last couple of decades. The unprecedented scale of globalization process has attracted global attention in recent years (OECD, 2008). Although economic integration is a predominant characteristic of globalization, other factors, for example social, cultural, political and institutional are also very significant. For some globalization is merely an economic and technological phenomenon for others it is an inevitable social and cultural force. Few see it a huge opportunity for economic progress and development and for others it is a threat to national sovereignty, independence integrity, self-determination of individual, cultural diversity and so on. However, many economic scholars argue that globalization is not a new phenomenon; it started from the days of long-distance trade, exploration, and conquest (Walsh, 2003). Organization for Economic Co-operation and Development (OECD) defines "globalization" as

> "…the increasing internationalization of financial markets and of markets for goods and services. Globalization refers above all to a dynamic and multidimensional process of economic integration whereby national resources become more and more internationally mobile while national

economies become increasingly interdependent" (OECD, 2005).

Famous economist Nobel Laureate Joseph Stiglitz defines globalization as

"...the closer integration of the countries and peoples of the world which has been brought about by the enormous reduction of costs of transportation and communication, and the breaking down of artificial barriers to the flows of goods, services, capital, knowledge, and (to a lesser extent) people across borders" (Stieglitz, 2002).

Whether, a proponent or opponent of globalization; everyone is unanimous on the fact that the Globalization is a potent force. This present force of globalization has affected national economy all over the globe in a remarkable way (Ohme, 1990). The three main channels of economic globalization in the present phase are; *trade, foreign direct investment (FDI)* and the *international knowledge and technology transfer*. All these three channels have developed very rapidly in the countries around the world (OECD, 2008). Using all these means, developed countries have made great economic progress by actively participating in the global economics. Following the developed countries' model recently, a group of developing countries has stepped into global economics (Zedillo, 2008). The process of economic integration is quickly taken pace and perhaps reached at its top in the last three decades.

In today's globalized world, *international trade* is growing faster than the world output. The degree of openness has reached a record level. Recent advancement in Information and Communication Technology (ICT) and the web technology in particular have lowered the communication cost, fueled the trade and economic globalization process very rapidly (OECD 2008). Multinational Enterprises (MNEs) are the crucial element of all these rapid changes. Therefore, MNEs are the key actor of all of these developments (Kleinert, 2001).

FDI expedites the international trade and transfer, knowledge, skills and technology. In the present world of increased competition and speedy technological change, their complimentary and catalytic role can be very valuable (Planning Commission, GOI 2002). Foreign Direct Investment (FDI) flows are usually favored than other forms of external finance by the host economics, because FDI is non-debt creating, non-volatile. Their returns depend on the performance of the projects financed by the investors. FDI by MNEs is a long-term process and the different aspects of internationalization are interrelated with each other based on the firm's strategy (Edwards, 2002).

Along with international trade and FDI, *international knowledge and technology transfer* happen across geographical borders without loss of time. This is perhaps, because of recent trade liberation and unprecedented technological changes globally. Previously, process and production function were located together. Now they are separate and placed apart to take cost advantage, logistics and market differences. Changes in location and organization take place under market force. Enterprises are taking up affiliate to manage production and trade under direct control through FDI in a highly coordinated system (Lall, 2003).

Role of MNEs in Globalization process

MNEs have huge global production networks and increasingly export intermediate and final goods between their foreign subsidiaries. Due to this increasing MNEs activities, growth of labour movement across borders has also increased and contributed significantly to international economic integration (OECD, 2008). Therefore, interest is MNEs and international business research has been advanced both by popular and scholarly fashion. At the policy level, different governments also seek to understand the role of MNEs in the new global economy and the possible government's role in the host and home country MNEs in shaping the world economic order

(Nicholas & Elizabeth, 2002). Because of trade liberalization enterprises are facing competition in domestic and international markets as well. Different low-cost communications medium and rapid technological changes forces enterprises to upgrade process technologies for introducing new products. It also changes trade pattern, and more R&D intensive products are increasingly coming into the market in place of less technology intensive segments (Lall, 2003). As, innovation is costly and risky affair, there is greater inter firm and cross-national collaboration and networking in innovation effort.

FDI by MNEs is spreading throughout world since last couple of decades. Many countries and industrial sectors are becoming the part of international FDI network. Different level and diverse forms of FDI by MNEs integrating world economy in unprecedented way perhaps never happened before. Recently a strong rise in FDI has attracted the global attention.

A new and more recent trend has been observed in the world scenario, that globalization has expanded beyond the Triad (the United States, the EU and Japan). The new global players like China, India, Brazil and Russia have also deeply integrated into the process. As OECD report observed, China and India in particular, have enormously increased the global labor supply at lower cost than the developed countries. The overall impact of globalization is also significant with these countries (OECD, 2008).

Internationalization vs. Globalization

Like Globalization, the Internationalization process is being explored extensively over the last few decades from different viewpoints. It is analyzed using concepts from economic, social, organizational, marketing, management and so on. Internationalization is the process of increasing involvement of firms in international operations. The term "Internationalization" is used to describe the dynamic phenomenon of increasing cross-border trade of goods and services and mobility of various production factors such as people and capital. It is the geographical expansion of a firm's economic activities beyond its national border. This phenome-non involves a number of interconnected and interdependent activities and actors through different formal and informal channels. The term "globalization" is sometimes used when internationalization has further deepened and encompasses a large number of countries worldwide and when the process has become increasingly separated from a particular home country of the parent company. According to Nicholas & Elizabeth (2002), 'Globalization' and 'Internationalization' are frequently misunderstood and misused terms. Internationalization and globalization differ from other growth strategies, such as product diversification, because they involve transacting in goods, services and know-how across national borders (Nicholas & Elizabeth, 2002). *There are no clear-cut distinctions between these two terms and sometimes both the terms are used interchangeably* (ITPS 2006). However, Narula, (2005) has made a distinction between these processes:

> Globalization is an ongoing process, rather than an event. Economic globalization implies the growing interdependence of locations and economic units across countries and regions. Cross-border linkages between economic entities do not imply globalization, merely internationalization (Narula, 2005, 2003).

Daly (1999)[1] from Global Policy Forum defines globalization as

> Globalization, considered by many to be the inevitable wave of the future, is frequently confused with internationalization, but is in fact something totally different. Internationalization refers to the increasing importance of international trade,

---

1 Global Policy Forum (GPF) is an independent policy watchdog that monitors the work of the United Nations and scrutinizes global policymaking. GPF works particularly on the UN Security Council, the food and hunger crisis, and the global economy. We promote accountability and citizen participation in decisions on peace and security, social justice and international law. Website http://www.globalpolicy.org/ accessed on 15th December 2020

international relations, treaties, alliances, etc. Inter-national, of course, means between or among nations. The basic unit remains the nation, even as relations among nations become increasingly necessary and important. Globalization refers to global economic integration of many formerly national economies into one global economy, mainly by free trade and free capital mobility, but also by easy or uncontrolled migration. It is the effective erasure of national boundaries for economic purposes. International trade (governed by comparative advantage) becomes interregional trade (governed by absolute advantage). What was many becomes one (Daly 1999).

Internationalization process requires a firm to adapt its resources, structure and organization to international environments. Investment, divestment growth and expansion, are the part of internationalization process. The term 'Internationalization' started used after World War I. Perhaps, this phenomenon gradually equated and replaced with imperialism. The economic internationalization process accelerated World War II and gradually replaced with the new term called "Globalization" (Ruzzier & Bostjan 2006). Globalization usually refers the firm's operations that are managed on a global scale rather than few selected countries. It is characterized by the worldwide integration of competitive markets and firms in global competitive market. Here corporate interest dominates over subunit maximization.

Globalization of business is boosted in recent years because of three major reasons (OECD, 2005). *Firstly*, the exponential growth is because of high technology available at low-cost particularly. These latest technologies are connecting people and locations at no time. These technologies are creating awareness and new business opportunities around the world. *Secondly*, many countries have adopted the free trade agreements and financial deregulation. *Thirdly*, the worldwide economic restructuring and liberalization has given it a tremendous boost. For example, the global business got momentum due to the collapse of socialism in Russia and few European countries.

Further there was an expansion of markets in developing Asia, particularly India and China. Despite all these driving forces of globalization, internationalization has not been replaced, rather, many observations and theories on internationalization persists and valid today (Ruzzier & Bostjan, 2006). In a globalizing economy, MNEs are the major drivers through which globalization has occurred and are developed. MNEs are the creator of new technologies. They are not only the generator of new technology but also the vehicles for technology transfer. By means of 'green filed' or 'brown field' investment and other forms of cross-border value-adding activity, MNEs usually transfer technology across borders (Dunning & Lundan, 2009). In today's globalized world, MNEs are gradually organizing themselves into cross-border international knowledge networks beyond their nationality.

Due to the intense global competition and the urgent need for strategic interactions, (*asset exploiting or asset augmenting*) (Kuemmerle 1999) MNEs are rapidly expanding beyond their geographical boundaries. This new trend of knowledge generation activity is observed during the last few decades. As mentioned earlier, advances in the transportation and communication technologies associated with globalization have enabled the spread of the value creating activities of MNEs on a global scale. Accordingly, the geography of the innovative activities of MNEs has radically changed. The knowledge generation activities of Multinationals are no longer encircled by distinct geographical boundary rather considerable proportion of knowledge created by MNEs is the result of their cross-border knowledge-generating activities. Dunning (2009) has observed three main trends in the patterns of the internationalization of the knowledge creating and knowledge sourcing activities of MNEs. *First*, the internationalization of the innovative activities of MNEs are increasing at an phenomenal rate still it is less preferred activity than the internationalization of production. *Second*, MNEs foreign subsidiaries are getting more autonomy in their R&D activity.

Third, the innovative activities of MNEs have become more geographically dispersed than before (Dunning & Lundan 2009).

Internationalization of R&D

Research on the nature and distribution of inward or outward R&D investment in developed countries are available since 1960s. The theories were mainly concentrated on internationalization of production. A separate set of literature exclusively deals with internationalization of R&D (Howells, 1990). Although there are several attempts to accommodate international production and internationalization of R&D in a unified approach (Dunning, 1977), like famous Production Life Cycle model and ownership, location, internalization (OLI) model sometimes used to explain the off-shoring of R&D process. However, the theories and literature on internationalization R&D has developed as a separate stream and can be regarded as separate discipline.

Archibugi & Michie (1999) have categorized the globalization of innovation into three main categories *the international exploitation of technology produced on a national basis; the global generation of innovations;* and *the global technological collaborations* (Archibugi & Iammarino 1999). Little & Veugelers (2005) found four main processes behind the internationalization of R&D. Both the public and private actors are involved to exploit the potential to benefit from international exchanges in terms of either research and training or access to technology. Internationalization of business R&D today is not only influencing the innovation and technology strategies of companies rather it enforces and changes the network of science around the world (Archibugi et al., 1999).

It is already discussed that, among the many other actors, MNEs that dominate global FDI flows. They are also the main source of innovation. They are also the crucial players in the National Innovation System (NIS) of both home and country. Because of their certain advantages, MNEs are the vital force in conducting cutting-edge research and innovation. In addition, international knowledge flows like, trade, licensing, cross-patenting activities, and international technological and scientific collaborations (Narula & Zanfei, 2005, Granstand et al., 1993) by many other ways.

Modern MNEs are the main driver and important channels for cross-border knowledge generation, flows and diffusion of innovation across national borders (Narula & Zanfei, 2005). MNEs control a vast proportion of world's scientific and technical resources. About 95 percent of the 700 firms spend close to half of the world's total R&D expenditure and more than two-thirds of the world's business R&D (UNCTAD, 2005). Many MNEs who are the largest spenders in R&D often spend more than many countries' total R&D budget (OECD 2008, van Bavel et al., 2006).

However, R&D has long been one of the least mobile activities of MNEs because of its complex and tacit nature (Pavitt & Patel, 1999, OECD, 2008). Firms usually perform R&D patenting at home because of fear of technological knowledge leakage. In addition, knowledge is not transferable because of its nature. It has 'tacit' part and often 'sticky' and embodied in location and persons. Therefore, it is not easily transferable. Moreover, firms' competitive advantage is often directly related to its strength in home country and as such is strongly shaped by that country's industrial specializations and national innovation systems, including its accumulated research and labor force skills (Pavitt and Patel, 1999).

Empirical evidences show that MNEs keep core innovative capabilities close to their home base (Patel & Pavitt, 1991). The study of technological activities of large firms outside their home country shows that firms firmly embedded in the condition of the technological strength in their home country. Patel & Vega (1999) studied the United States Patent data of 220 of the most internationalized firms. Their findings showed that, most of the firms tend to locate their technology abroad in their core areas where they are strong at home. Firms also engaged in small-scale activities to monitor and scan new technological developments in centers of excellence in foreign countries within their areas of existing strength. Even the most internationalized firms rarely go abroad to compensate for their weakness at home (Patel & Vega, 1999). Firms, keep R&D activities at home because a R&D unit located close to headquarter can easily be communicated and coordinated (WIR 2005). Above all firm can easily coordinate with the governmental bodies and can keep their R&D activity secret without leaking it to potential rivals (Niosi, 1997). Despite such obstacles, off shoring of R&D by multinational is increasing. Many evidences (UNCTAD 2005, OECD 2008) showed that the top spenders on R&D have increasingly invested in R&D outside their home country. The United Nations Conference on Trade and Development UNCTAD (2005) survey found that among the responding firms 69 percent stated that their share of foreign R&D would increase in future. European Commission study also finds similar result; nearly 70 percent of the companies had increased their R&D off shoring over the last couple of years (OECD 2008).

Although there are strong forces for centralization of R&D in home country, decentralization of R&D seems an inherent in the growth and evolution of MNEs. Håkanson & Nobel (1993) identified three possible reasons for increasing share of foreign R&D over time. These reasons are *Acquisition*, *Greenfield investment*, *Exploitation of foreign R&D resources*.

Evolution of Global R&D

Internationalization of R&D was not the important research topic for scholars until the early 1980's among government policy and decision-making bodies even among the scholars. Except a few expressed the concern and noticed that, the overseas R&D activities of US-based firms may hollow out the national technological capability (Mansfield et al., 1979). However, by the 1990s it had become an important subject because of empirical evidence. These evidences were mainly backed by three types of data, patenting activity by foreign affiliates, the geographical distribution of the R&D expenditures of MNEs, and survey-based evidence on the question of R&D location (Dunning & Lundan 2009, Niosi, 1999). A new trend observed by different researchers that in late 80's there was the rapid increase in foreign-funded and foreign-performed R&D in most industrialized countries. *OECD Science and Technology Indicators Report* and the *United States National Science Board Science and Engineering Indicators* reported in early 1990s, observed that there was an acceleration in the internationalization of industrial R&D (Niosi 1999; Cheng & Bolon 1993; NSF 1990).

With that new trend, the new research trends open up with new theoretical framework and hypothesis. Many scholars challenged the previous notions of foreign R&D centers. Studies had confirmed that MNE's foreign R&D laboratories were not only confined themselves to adapting parent company technology to host countries, but gradually evolved to develop major innovations for catering the needs of global market. Previously, MNEs overseas R&D largely involved adapting products and services to the local need. Beside this, R&D activities were also a supporting to the MNEs' local manufacturing operations.

Different scholars (Reddy 1997, Hegde & Hicks 2008, Niosi 1999, Cantwell & Piscitello 2000, Dunning & Lundan 2009) have identified the different phases of internationalization of R&D firms. These studies have provided theoretical and empirical insights into techno-economic, social, impact of foreign R&D centers in the innovation system. Moreover, those studies also investigated the motivations, conditions, influences, and interactions among different actors in a national innovation system (NIS). Few studies also investigated the issues of knowledge spillovers (Reddy 1997, Niosi 1999; Hedge & Hicks, 2008). Moreover, those works showed that, the dominant type of foreign R&D in a country depends on technological capability, economic, social and political configurations.

Today, MNEs are not only exploiting knowledge generated at home in other countries, but also to source technology internationally and tap into worldwide centers of knowledge. This technology scouting process was more prevalent among Triad region and among developed countries MNEs. Although internationalization of R&D is not entirely new, previously it was more prevalent among Triad Nations (US, Europe and Japan), in recent years it is taking place in an unprecedented way and at a much faster pace than before (OECD, 2008). However, the current web of internationalization of R&D is markedly different from the earlier phase. OECD (2008) report observed that the present internationalization as: *it is gathering pace*, it is all *invasive* and *spreading* to more and more countries, including developing countries, and it goes beyond adapting technology to local conditions. Dunning (2009) has also observed that internationalization of the knowledge creating and knowledge sourcing activities of MNEs are increasing at a phenomenal rate beyond their national origin. However, it still a less preferred activity than the internationalization of production (Dunning & Lundan, 2009). In addition, in the 1980s, foreign R&D was mainly a developing country phenomenon and FDI in R&D usually took place between the triads (i.e., United States, Europe and Japan). However, with the present wave of globalization large upcoming and promising countries like India and China are rapidly integrated with the global value chain.

Global Research Trends

The internationalization of R&D is the process where multinational distributes their R&D activities around the globe to leverage its innovation capability. Globalization of R&D is considered as the more mature form of Internationalization encompassing more in-depth and significant amount of R&D carried out by firms in different centers dispersed in different places globally. There are vast amounts of literature available on its various aspect of it, a selected few is presented in the table 2.1 below:

Table 5. Major literature of interest in Internationalization R&D

THEORETICAL FRAMEWORK

Area	Issues	Major works
Management of R&D subsidiary	These studies mainly dealt with firms' site selection, autonomy of their subsidiaries, coordination and control in organizational structure, human resource management in R&D units.	Cheng (1993), Ronstad (1977), Behrman and Fischer (1980), Hakanson & Zander (1988), Ghoshal and Bartlett's (1988), De Meyer & Mizushima's (1989), Chiesa (1996), Asakawa (2001), Chiesa (1996), Westney (1997). Cheng&Bolon (1993)
Typologies of different foreign R&D units	Geographical locations, types of R&D performed by MNE subsidiaries,	Ronstadt (1977), Hood & Young (1982), Pearce (1989), Bartlett & Ghoshal (1989), Hakanson (1993), Archibugi & Michie (1995), Chiesa (1996), Nobel & Birkinshaw (1998), Gerybadze & Reger (1999), Kuemmerale (1999), Niosi & Godin (1999), Patel & Vega (1999), Zander (1999), Gassmann & von Zedtwitz (1999), Gassmann & von Zedtwitz (2002), Sachwald (2008)
R&D Globalization process	The studies mainly dealt with the whole country as a case study,	De Meyer and Mizushima (1989), De Meyer (1992), Westney (1993), Hedlund and Ridderstrale (1994), Kenney and Florida (1994) Patel (1995), Florida (1997), Gerybadze et al. (1997), Kuemmerle (1997)
R&D Globalization and its implications	Literature mainly dealt with the effect of (technology transfer, Knowledge spillover, Capacity building) R&D internationalization process from developing and developed country's perspective	Mansfield (1975), Mansfield et al (1979), Teece (1977), Reddy (2005), Narula (2005), Blomström & Kokko (1998), Pearce (1997),

The strategic management of technology of the world's most technology-intensive companies from Triad regions

29

(Western Europe, North America and Japan) observed that R&D and technology is the key cornerstones of corporate and business strategy. There is a growing tendency to acquire technology from external sources among the MNEs. As a result, foreign of R&D plays important role in the strategies of the large companies (Edler et al., 2002). MNEs reformulating their global strategies with the increasing decentralized R&D units. In the first line of strategies, the new globalized approach to innovation is to develop new or variant products, for key segments of the global marketplace. In the second line, dispersed labs may take specialized and basic research depends on the host-country's science or technology strength. Decentralized R&D units are increasingly becoming important compete the global environment, i.e., *market* and *technological heterogeneity* (Pearce & Papanastassiou, 1999). The impact of overseas subsidiaries' R&D activities on the productivity growth of parent firms shows that overseas innovative R&D raises the parent firm's productivity. The adaptive R&D does not have any productivity growth as such. Above all, overseas innovative R&D does not improve the rate of return on home R&D (Iwasa & Odagiri 2004, Todo & Shimizutani 2008). Kumar (2001) observed that overseas R&D activity of Japanese MNEs and US mainly concentrated on overseas market, where there is low-cost R&D work force available, and the scale of national technological effort is suitable for augment the MNEs technology strength. The study also further confirmed that a significant proportion of MNEs' R&D activity follows that of leaders in their own fields 'sector-wise'.

Edlar 2002 observed that, until the first half of 21st century R&D was confined to the Triad regions only and was not a true 'global' phenomenon (Edler et al., 2002). Reddy (1997) observed that, since the mid-1980s, MNEs had started performing some of their strategic R&D in some developing countries (Reddy, 1997). The reports World Investment Report (WIR 2005) and many scholarly works observed that R&D internationalization has increasingly involved countries outside the developed world

(Chen, 2007). This may be considered as global phenomenon and the more mature form as "Globalization of R&D"

There are increasing foreign activity by MNEs in developing countries particularly in India and China. Beside these, East Asia countries like Singapore, Taiwan, are becoming attractive locations for the R&D facilities of MNEs. This new and emerging trend in the mobility and geography of R&D processes by MNEs had raised the question of whether there is a fundamental *paradigm shift* in globalization of R&D (Bruche, 2009). Also, question is being raised that this recent trends R&D will lead to the *'destruction'* of the *'the iron cage of the triad'* (Chen, 2007), and possibly mark the beginning of a shift in the global hierarchy of knowledge and power (Chen, 2007, Bruche, 2009).

Costs and Benefits of global R&D

A number of studies are available on the impact of MNEs' R&D activities on the host country. However, most of the studies are from the developed country's perspective to look into the positive and negative effect of foreign R&D. There is a strong debate on the impact of foreign R&D on the home and host country. Scholars have difference of opinion on the subject (Granstand et al. 1993). Some argue that impact is positive while other says that it is negative. Whether, the R&D by MNE in host country enhance or retard the technological capability of the host country is a complicated issue (Reddy, 2005). However, it is universally accepted that, MNE's R&D activities related to product development for regional/global markets and generic technologies diffuse skills and knowledge to the host countries.

It is well established in the literature and widely accepted fact that, MNEs are the key actor of globalization process and important sources of capital and technology. The economic growth of every nation is linked to the successful international technology transfer (Teece, 1977). Therefore, the foreign R&D by MNEs are always a hot debated topic from both home and host country's perspective. The impact of foreign R&D centers on the home and host country may be many. The scholars like Mansfield, Teece and Williamson stressed, on the hypothesis that MNEs are the relatively efficient mechanism for transferring technology. Their work strongly supports the theory that the MNEs can be an instrument of economic development (Teece, 2005). From the home country's view outward FDI in R&D may 'hollowing out' the domestic innovation capability and the job loss. However, in the positive side, the firms foreign R&D operation in 'foreign centers of excellence' to acquire global stock of technical knowledge may have 'spillover effect' in the home country. From the developing country's perspective, MNE's knowledge creation by means of foreign R&D has lots of positive as well as negative impact. Scholars have difference of opinion on the subject (Reddy, 2005; Granstand et al., 1993; Reddy, 1997). Some argue that impact is positive while other says that it is negative. However, the positive aspect of MNEs R&D activity in the host country outweigh than the negative aspects. Granstand et al (1993) analyzed impact of foreign R&D depends on the type of R&D and the benefit MNEs incurred (Narula, 2005).

During the 1980's many host countries have relaxed their FDI rules regulations to encourage foreign invest and to reap the benefits of inward FDI. For the positive side FDI in R&D is considered the beneficial to economic growth and general welfare. FDI helps in capital formation, employment generation, international exports, and technological capability building (Blomström, & Kokko, 1998). In addition, countries try to attract foreign investment to acquire modern technology, and skill sets associated with it, which perhaps host countries do not have owned. Foreign investment can be beneficial to the host country even the MNEs operate in the host country with 'wholly owned subsidiary'. Because knowledge is a public good and different types of positive externalities called, 'productivity spillover' occurs because of MNEs foreign operations (Blomström & Kokko, 1998). MNEs represent an alternative to traditional technology transfer approaches to promote the competitiveness among the domestic firms in the host country. It may develop forward or backward linkage with the foreign firms and may hire trained workers from the foreign firms. It may assist the foreign subsidiary to improve product and export performance. With their enriched experience of global market, domestic firms may try to enter into the global market through 'market access spillover'. With a link with the host, country's S&T community the foreign R&D centre may help in developing technological capability of the host country. From the consumers' side the local R&D improves the local manufacturing by adapting products and processes to the local conditions. As a result, the products are available at low cost. In the negative side; R&D activities by foreign firms has a tendency to tap local R&D resources with little or no benefit to the host country. Sometimes, R&D activity concentrated on problems that are not at all applicable to the local condition. However, in the developing country's context the benefits are larger because over the long-term knowledge (because of its public good character) and skills cannot be isolated. The mobility of researchers and linkages with the different local actors along the value chain are bound to diffuse technologies throughout the host economy (Reddy, 2005).

R&D activities of MNEs generate widespread benefits to the consumers and society. The result of foreign R&D often adds great economic value to society. It often surpasses the economic benefits incurred by the innovating firms. *Economists as a positive externality or spillover (Jaffe, 1996) describe this excess of the social rate of return over the private rate of return enjoyed by innovating firms.* Although there is no direct and comprehensive evidence of spillover effects of the activities of multinational firms in the host countries, but the operations of foreign MNEs may influence local firms of the same industry as well as firms in other industries. However, the positive effects of foreign investment in R&D depend on the local capability and competition (Reddy, 1997, Blomström, & Kokko, 1998, Reddy,

2005). Blomström & Kokko (1998) identified two kinds of spillover; *productivity spillover* and *market spillover* MNE differ from the local firms in the way that they possess unique propriety knowledge that gives them firms' specific advantage. On the other hand, local firms have better knowledge about the local market. To compensate this MNEs use their 'firm specific knowledge' and international experience to compete with them. Therefore, the entries of MNE into a local market disturb the existing equilibrium. This likely to cause various types of spillovers and ultimately leads to productivity increase in local firms (Blomström & Kokko, 1998). Jaffe (1996) identified three distinct channels of knowledge spillover. First, *market spillovers*, which arise as a result of markets for innovative products which benefits consumers and non-innovating firms. Second, *knowledge spillovers*; because of public good nature of knowledge. It may not be restricted to a firm rather it can create value to others. Finally, the *network spillover*; interrelationship among firms on interdependent technologies create economic benefits for other firms and their customers (Jaffe, 1996).

Impact of foreign R&D unit on the developing host economy and innovation system is based on the types of R&D unit established (Pearce, 1997). R&D laboratory of an MNE operate in a foreign country is to help the subsidiary. These units used to enhance the MNE's current technology embodied in existing products and services effectively. Its main function is, therefore for the adaptation for the local customers' needs. Subsidiaries with these functions are termed as *Support Laboratories* (SL). Reddy has categories the potential impact of R&D-related FDI on a developing host country (examples were drawn from Indian case) can be classified into *direct effects, spin-off effects* and *spillover effects* (Reddy, 2005).

The new trend of FDI in R&D may offer new opportunities for developing host countries. R&D investments are opening up new employment opportunities and international prestige. In addition, international R&D may encourage indigenous firms to perform their own R&D. However, to grab the opportunity, 'readiness' of the host country is important (Reddy, 2005). As more and more R&D centers are being allowed to operate in in developing countries, researchers assumed that developing countries would be benefited in the grey areas. Linkages between the local innovation systems and MNEs' worldwide R&D network, helps to integrate developing countries into global technology development activities (Reddy, 1997). The presence of foreign R&D centers can trigger the spillover effect onto the host country's innovation system depending on the ability, preparedness and conducive policy of the host country (Cohen & Levinthal 1990, Granstand et al., 1999; Mody, 2007; Mrinalini & Wakdikar, 2008).

Under this theoretical framework, the Chapter VII will deal with the linkage and possible knowledge spill over form the presence of MNEs R&D centre in India and China. The chapter will present the selected case studies of joint R&D, joint development and training programs imparted by MNEs in India and China.

Motivation and Driving Forces

The main motive behind investment in foreign R&D are technology-related, (i.e., to gain access to S&T resources) and cost-related, (i.e., to exploit the difference in cost). With the rapid globalization process in the last few decades, it is realized that knowledge is the most important source of competitiveness, innovation and development. Globalization and the increasing economic importance of knowledge, dispersed globally, have given rise to a recent trend towards increasing internationalizetion of firm. Although, firms have internationalized their sales and manufacturing activities, since long, the internationalization of R&D is a more recent phenomenon. For knowledge generation, acquisition and diffusion firms increasingly internationalize their core activities like R&D. MNEs are usually retain their R&D in the home country for a variety of reasons including fear of leaking secrets to competitors, embeddedness in a particular knowledge cluster or near to university and so on.

Although, MNEs generally retained R&D close to headquarters in their home country, their science, technology and innovation processes are today increasingly dispersed geographically across the value chain (Gammeltoft, 2006). Innovation has major consequences for a firm's economic performance. However, not all firms can get benefits from innovation. Firms need to have a sufficient degree of internationalization to reap benefit through innovation. However, firms are cannot get benefit from innovation if their international activity is below a threshold level (Kafouros et. al., 2008).

Although, MNE performs most of their R&D activity in the home country a number of recent studies have found that foreign R&D by MNEs is increasing to exploit benefit from foreign R&D. The decision to locate R&D is quite complex and influenced by a variety of factors (Thursby & Thursby, 2006). Overseas R&D in MNEs is in response to both demand side and supply side factors. On the demand side, laboratories can help to adapt or develop products for a particular market (demand-side factor). R&D laboratories may be located where the good scientific inputs are available (supply-side factor). Therefore, the location of this is even more likely to be influenced by countries' scientific capabilities and capacities (Pearce, 1994). Drawing upon Boddewyn's (1985) work, Cheng & Bolon (1993) classified three important factors responsible for increasing multinational R&D. These are *conditions*, *motivations*, and *precipitating circumstances*.

The development in ICT, globally interconnected economics, uniform patent rule are the *conditions* that make foreign R&D possible or economically rational. Investing in foreign R&D firms could get return in terms of higher innovation output or lower operating cost. Scientific talents, new ideas, location specific international division of labor, market need, host government encouragements in various forms are motivation factors. *Precipitating circumstances* reflect actions both inside and outside of the firm, which make the firms to invest abroad. Participating circumstances include technical support to local market, competitor's R&D investment abroad, shortage of R&D workers in home country, host government pressure for investment in R&D, center of excellence dispersed globally. Literature on internationalization of R&D of last decades concentrated on the various push, pull factors to explain the phenomenon and found that internationalizetion of R&D is location dependent, and government policy has significant role (Granstand, et. al., 1993).

The drivers behind and consequence of FDI in R&D and the link to the economic development is a complex and difficult task. The motive behind FDI is a combination of various factors (Lundvall, 2008). Although there are many motives behind the investment in foreign countries by MNEs, the motives can be broadly categories into three types. These are *market seeking, resource seeking and efficiency-seeking* (UNCTAD, 2007). However, some other factors such as host country business environment is also important. Gammeltoft (2006) categorized six types of motives for foreign R&D: *market-driven, production-driven, technology-driven, innovation-driven, cost-driven and policy-driven* (Gammeltoft, 2006).

Foreign R&D by MNEs is subject to different location drivers. Von Zedtwitz & Gassmann (2002) observed that research is concentrated in only few concentrated pockets worldwide, while development is more globally dispersed (von Zedtwitz & Gassmann, 2002). The geographical location of R&D by MNEs has been analyzed in terms of two competing and contradictory forces i.e., 'Centrifugal forces' (decentralization) and 'Centripetal forces' (centralization) (Chiesa, 1996).

Several empirical surveys and case studies have found the motivation and determinants of decentralization of R&D. For example, a survey of about 200 multinationals by *Thrusby & Thrusby* (2006) from 15 industries group found four major factors viz: *output market potential, quality of R&D personnel, university collaboration,* and *intellectual property protection*. However, in emerging economics, major attraction for MNEs for offshore

R&D, is the local market potential followed by the high quality of R&D personnel. They further observed that, the host government's incentives in the form of tax break, and the ease of collaboration with universities is important factor for offshoring R&D. For developing countries, the intellectual property protection is an important issue and may act as detracting factor.

Although, Booz & Company and INSEAD Survey (Doz et al., 2006) found the traditional drivers like proximity to market and production facility is still the most important driver of R&D globalization. High skilled work force ranked second in developing countries. However, the drivers highly differentiated across region. The study further predicted that growth in the developing world would be motivated by "low-cost skills base" and "access to markets and customers". The major finding of the study was that in India, the highly qualified R&D staff attract firms. However, firms are attracted to China because of potential Chinese market and low-cost skills base.

During the second half of 1980's, Japanese firms actively engaged in overseas R&D activity mainly to support local marketing (Odagiri & Yasuda, 1996). Later, the Japanese multinationals' R&D activities abroad showed that the basic and applied research base of overseas subsidiaries used to exploit foreign advanced knowledge. However, host country's market size was the determining factor for the development and design activities (Shimizutani & Todo, 2008). The study of Edler (2004) on German and Non-German MNEs operating in Germany observed that, the market adaptation of products was the major driver for German firms, but international knowledge seeking was increasingly important, especially in technological areas that were linked to basic research. Germany as a host of international industrial R&D was much more attractive for applied research (mechanical engineering) than for basic research (Edler, 2004). MNEs located their activities abroad in technological areas or fields where they were strong at home. However, it differed depend upon the MNEs country of origin.

THEORETICAL FRAMEWORK

For Example, the strategy of Japanese firms was quite different from European and US MNEs. Japanese firms established their operation in the locations where they had complementary strengths of their own (Le Bas & Sierra, 2002). However, the World Investment Report (WIR, 2005) found India and China as the most attractive location in terms investment. China was considered the most attractive location by 85 percent of MNEs and experts.

Regarding the location of R&D centers at the sub national scale, two types of models have been proposed: the *rational choice model* and the *imitating behavior model* (Sun et al., 2006, Sun & Wen, 2007). According to rational choice theory firms choose, R&D locations after considering *internal* organizational and managerial factors. As a result, it is generally observed that firms prefer to keep R&D near the headquarters (Sun et al., 2006).

The literature of knowledge creation in multinational corporations, observed that the location of foreign-owned research tends to agglomerate depending upon the potential of different sources of spillovers and externalities. These factors have been categorized based on the proximity of the source of knowledge. Cantwell and Piscitello (2005) have classified the external factors into three major groups. *Firstly, the intra-industry spillovers or specialization externalities* where firms of the same sectors co-located in the same place to reap benefit of the same location advantage. *Secondly; inter-industry spillovers or diversity externalities* where firms working in the different fields present together in the same location to be benefited from spillover in different level of the value chain. *Finally; Science-technology spillovers and externalities* which mainly arises because of the universities, research institutions, other knowledge centers and suitable educational infrastructure (Cantwell & Piscitello, 2005, Sun et al., 2006).

Under the theoretical framework on motivation of firms, the chapter IV will examine various motives of firms to open their R&D centers in India and China. The chapter will deal will the various motivation for example, local market global market, talent size, or general expansion and so on.

Globalization of R&D from developing country's perspective

Internationalization or even globalization of R&D has become a buzzword in technology policy discussion circles in recent years. As discussed earlier, a rapid internationalization of R&D is being observed, both on macro scale (i.e., the share of R&D financed by abroad) and on micro scale (i.e., the amount of R&D carried out abroad by MNEs) (Gassl & Brigitte, 2008). Globalization is opening new opportunities for knowledge creation and dissemination. However, this globalization process can only benefit institutions, which are at the core of scientific and technological advance, if they implement active policies designed to increase learning and improve access to knowledge and technology (Archibugi & Pietrobelli, 2003). In this context, the innovation systems approach can guide government policy in several ways. Today, the sources of knowledge are often located outside the national boundaries. The policy issues related to System of Innovation (SI) deals with various level and different sets of policies are required to access knowledge outside the Innovation System (Archibugi & Michie, 1999). For example, one sets of policy deals with the organizations, which generates innovation and the interactions between various actors, associated with them. Other sets of policy may deal with institutions like standards, patents IPR and so on.

In case of foreign technology, either embodied or disembodied, has a negligible learning impact. These foreign technologies must be accompanied by local policies to promote learning, develop human capital and technological capabilities. Public policies should therefore try to induce foreign firms to move from exporting their products to producing it locally. It is also more advantageous for a developing country to set up inter-firm strategic technological agreements rather than simply hosting production facilities of foreign firms. Public policies should therefore also try to "upgrade" FDI to strategic technological collaborating. Collaborations among public and business organizations can provide substantial benefits to developing countries. Policies at both the national and intergovernmental levels should therefore consider these collaborations as a preferential channel to transfer and acquire technological competencies (Archibugi & Pietrobelli 2003).

From the developing countries perspective, the following issues is important for the development of an effective System of Innovation. Linkages between industry and academia are an important aspect of good innovation practices worldwide. In a market economy, one of the most admired economic instruments for spurring innovation is venture capital. This form of support helps to reduce the "capital gap" faced by small entrepreneurs. Among the many successful examples, the growth of Silicon Valley as well as Taiwan and Israel are the famous examples of the intensive use of venture funds. The protection of IPRs is becoming important in knowledge-based economies. This is being driven by the escalating costs of R&D for new products or processes, short product life cycle, rapid growth in international trade in high-tech products, and internationalization of the research process (Aubert, 2005, Dahlman & Utz, 2005).

National S&T-policy can respond the growing phenomenon of foreign of R&D in various ways. National S&T-policy makers should encourage their country more scientifically and technologically. This can be achieved through special fiscal incentives like tax breaks, R&D tax credits and so on. Direct financial support may also be given to enhance national knowledge creation as well as to attract foreign R&D capabilities. In addition, the infrastructure such as the science parks and high-tech clusters are promoted, providing access to a science system that maintains both a highly developed infrastructure and excellent human resources by proximity (Gassler & Nones, 2008). However, this approach mainly focus on NIS is now changing, and emphasis is given to other levels like at regional, local, sectoral, and technology levels. This kind of approach is relevant because, policies designed and implemented at the supra-national level perhaps cannot address the local or regional level. For example, policies formulated from the developed countries' perspective may not reflect the needs of regional or sectoral level. At the same time, differences in types of innovation, as well as the organization of innovative activities in different business sectors, are demanding different policies. Finally, thinking in terms of innovation systems changes the focus of analysis from the internal working of an economic system (whether countries, regions or national sectors), to the way that the system interacts with the outside world. Similarly, international institutions, such as the Agreement on Trade-Related Aspects of Intellectual Property Rights (TRIPS) of the World Trade Organization, influence the research and development decisions of firms in any national systems of countries that are members of the organization (Dantas, 2008). In sum Innovation system can be strengthen by increasing linkages with university and industry; solidification of intellectual property rights and; venture capital; promoting R&D by companies; encouraging new R&D niches.

Foreign R&D and Capacity building

Technology development is crucial for any country's development. Developing countries usually do not develop technology rather import technology from technologically advanced countries. Less developed countries, need to learn the use of technology effectively in order to develop. This is not an easy and simple process. Rather it is an incremental learning and cumulative process. Technology has lots of tacit part embedded in it. Hence, the capacity building is necessary. Technological capability building process put stress on building infrastructure, human resources, skill and above all a healthy synergy among or between these elements. However, technology diffusion in developing country is relatively easy as not all knowledge is tacit and market is efficient. Thus, developing countries can import and apply existing knowledge available in worldwide technology market with their factor price. Endogenous growth theories suggest that openness to trade and investment is sufficient and necessary. Free international trade and investment flows maximized the influence of beneficial knowledge.

Sanjaya Lall (Lall 2003) has argued that the above approach is very simplified. International technology market is not perfect. Beside this use of technology efficiently is not easy, costless and automatic. Technology is not sold in embodied form and its tacit element need effort and time to internalize. Although, capacity-building process is essential for both developed and developing countries, it is difficult for the developing countries. Learning to use new technologies needs investment and continuous efforts. Capacity building is difficult for developing countries because they have the weak infrastructure, market and institutions. In addition, mustering new technology is not a one-time investment. The learning process is uncertain, has lots of externalities, agglomeration, path dependent and cumulative effect. Moreover, technology capability building is a process and it requires time, investment and above all is uncertain.

System of Innovation (SI) approach as a framework of innovation is already popular and getting ground in developed countries. Although there are no definite blueprints for these complex tasks, however, innovation system approach can prescribe guidelines, such as the importance of capacity building in the business sector and supporting research organizations, promoting inter-organizational linkages, and encouraging a continuous feedback between institutions engaged in research, development, engineering, production and marketing. As a prescriptive tool, it provides a way of designing policies that respond to the specific needs of developing countries at different stages of their development. For example, it may identify a need at various stages to develop organizations or infrastructure to increase capability building in a country.

However, this concept is yet to become popular in developing countries. Care must have been taken before adoption of SI approach from developing countries as it is. The socioeconomic and demographic condition of developing countries are significantly different than the developed countries, a careful look perhaps is needed while applying this concept in developing countries perspectives (Dantas, 2008).

Innovation and Network

The increasing complexity in innovation process requires more collaboration and coordination among the different actors in the innovation process. This complexity is perhaps resulting in a new identifiable generation. Nebelius (2004) predicted a new generation of innovation management with more radical shift form the fifth generation. He termed it as *sixth generation* of R&D management. The new generation of R&D processes will be dominated by innovations that are more radical. Using the *Bluetooth technology* as case study, he predicted that the broader multi-technology base for high-tech products will dominate new generation of technology and more distributed technology-sourcing structure. Sixth generation of R&D management is expected to re-focus the research part, to augment the capabilities by connecting to loosely couple multi-technology research networks. There will be a range of multi-technology research networks available, e.g., corporate research labs, internal corporate venturing, technology company acquisitions, intellectual property acquisitions, corporate venture capital, joint ventures, independent research groups or networks, and internally driven R&D.

The systematic handling and assimilation of external knowledge resources is another key feature of fifth generation R&D management. The growth of collaborative activity is taken by means of the growing interdependence of locations and economic units across countries and regions are greatly influenced by the globalization process (Narula, 2003). Throughout the five identified R&D generations, the complexity associated with R&D management has continually expanded. Many complexities are interoperability, industrial design, environmental, manufacturability, and after-market considerations. As a result, inter-organizational network has grown considerably in recent past as network exposes a firm to access novel ideas, fast access to resources, and enhance technology transfer.

R&D Networks

Although, the network approach is not new but its use in innovation process was limited. The heterogeneous groups of contacts and its usefulness, originated form three different schools of thought *i.e* sociology, anthropology and role theory. By definition inter-organizational network means *"...by which organization can pool or exchange resources, and jointly develop new ideas and skills."* Tichy et al defined network analysis *"...is one method of conceptualizing organizations that captures the intersection of both static and dynamic aspects of organizations by focusing on the linkages between social objects over time"* (Tichy, 1979).

The advantage of network is well established in both social theory and network analysis. A well-established stream of literature (started from Merton 1957 and Granovetter, 1973) finds the usefulness in terms of infrastructure, information and other resources shearing. Although, sociological school of network perspective is old enough, but the studies on the relationship between network and innovation is comparatively new. Most of the studies emphasized on the high technology firms and their joint patenting as a means of knowledge shearing activity (Powell & Stine, 2006). In the similar line, many works have been available on the subject. However, there are very few studies available on networking of innovation activities or diffusion of innovation (Freeman, 1991). In addition, the relation between network ties and the financial performance of firms are relatively rare (Powell & Stine, 2006).

In the early 1960's research found that the external sources (for example; scientific, technical and market information) have a major role in successful innovation by business firms. Collaboration among ostensible rivals was once regarded as temporary phases for entering a new market (Powell & Stine, 2006). Later, such transitory alliances may become incorporated inside the boundaries of the firms by mergers or acquisitions. Studies confirmed that inter-organizational partnerships are increasingly becoming the new core concept of the corporate strategy. These collaborations can take a number of forms (research consortia, joint venture, strategic alliances, subcontracting and so on. Through various forms of partnerships, firms are tapping knowledge from a wide range of external partners like universities, research institutes, and even customers. Presently, complex network of firms' universities and government research laboratories are critical feature of many industries. However, the cooperation is particularly intense in high technology and capital-intensive sectors. Firms of high technology sectors in particular, need to innovate constantly to survive. These are sectors where firms have expanded internationally fastest, not only to compete in the various markets simultaneously, but also to exploit and acquire location specific assets and technology. In high technology sectors, particularly in pharmaceutical and ICT research units therefore has a leading role in firm's strategy and formulation of long-term corporate goals. However, firms or organizations do not necessarily possess all resources required for new knowledge or discoveries. Hence firms finding it necessary to corporate or form alliance with other organizations with similar or dissimilar activity in order to gain access to external creativity and new knowledge. With the growth of knowledge intensive industries, the network in R&D is becoming crucial. Beside this, to meet the demand and overcome supply constraints, firms need to be present in all global market. With the resource constraints and uncertain nature of innovation, it is not possible for firms to present in every global market. So, firms prefer for cooperative agreements to access location-specific resources. Such arrangements are useful organizational mode for firms to seek technologies that are specific to other firms (Narula & Duysters, 2004). Therefore, in high technology sectors, firms

THEORETICAL FRAMEWORK

find R&D alliances as a best option in many cases. Because of the similarity of technologies across geographical boundaries and cross-fertilization of technology between sectors, coupled with the increasing costs and risks associated with innovation there is a global trend in increasing R&D alliances (Narula & Duysters, 2004). However, in present day globalized world, firms moving from the older paradigm of *hierarchical capitalism* to the age of *alliance capitalism* (Narula & Duysters, 2004). As per definition, *"...alliance capitalism refers to the growing use of non-market, quasi-hierarchical modes of corporate activity, whereby firms do not completely (or formally) internalize their value-added activities, but utilize a variety of cooperative and collaborative agreements with other firms as a means to augment their own competitive advantage"*(Narula & Dunning, 1998). In the *'the age of alliance capitalism'* cooperative activity is not only limited to related firms but also sometimes undertaken with international competitors. Sometimes alliance is also gradually shifting from equity-based collaborating to no equity forms of agreements (Narula & Duysters, 2004). Firms usually prefer a full equity control in its affiliates particularly in foreign market. However, firms seek collaborative agreements when full internalization was not possible. So, alliances and networks are become the more popular options for firms in "alliance capitalism". Narula & Duyster 2004 characteristics present day alliance and networks as; *Firstly*, they are not primarily made to overcome market failure, *secondly*, alliances are not limited to just to achieve *vertical integration*, but also to achieve *horizontal integration*. *Thirdly*, alliances are not limited to certain countries, but it is increasingly gaining popularity among the MNEs of most advanced industrialized economies, *finally,* alliances are now made to protect or enhance the technological assets of firms. A number of literatures in this line clearly indicate that firms are able to increase their innovative capabilities by the use of strategic technology alliances (Narula & Duysters, 2004). Due to global competition and rapid technological changes, it is essential for firms and organizations to engage in uninterrupted innovation activity. As a result, R&D units are always expected to come up with new knowledge and discoveries at a very rapid place. Internal R&D intensity and technological capability are positively correlated with both the number and intensity of strategic alliances. Organizations in rapidly developing fields' heterogeneous collaborations allow firms to learn from a wide stock of knowledge (Powell & Stine, 2006). Exchange of new ideas or knowledge can be optimized when firms are aliened in a network (Suarez-Villa, 2002). Networks contribute significantly to the firm's innovative capabilities in R&D, along with the many other corporate activities, like sales, marketing etc. (Powell & Stine, 2006). Hagedoorn (2002) explores 40 years of data on R&D partnerships since 1960's among 'Triad' regions found that cooperation is the best option, rather than majority control. A recent joint survey by Booz & Company and INSEAD found that highly dispersed companies had higher levels of collaboration with research Institutes and universities (Doz, 2006). In addition, it is a general trend among the highly dispersed firms to have more joint ventures with local companies. It is easier to manage partnerships by dispersed companies, because they have close physical proximity to their local partner. Because of this reason, dispersed firms are in more advantageous position than the non-dispersed firms are. To sum up, networks can become locus of innovation, as the creation of knowledge is crucial to improving competitive position (Hagedoorn et al., 2000).

Modes of Alliances

From the economists' perspective, continuous innovation is regarded as crucial factor for productivity, growth and the competitive performance of firms, industries or nations. As, innovation is costly and risky affair, there is greater inter firm and cross-national collaboration and networking in innovation effort. However, successful innovation in inter-firm alliance networks depends upon the pattern of control and linkage (Freeman 1991). Some networks are hierarchical, monitored by central authority, while others are more flat organization with more autonomy and distributed authority (Powell & Stine, 2006).

For a successful innovation, both *formal* and *informal* networks are important. It is difficult to measure the impact of informal ties in innovation process. Although, it is not measured properly, rather systematically, scholars had given more weight to *informal* networks. Informal collaboration with the universities, government laboratories, different research groups, consultants, or even rival firms could be multiple sources of information. Thus, the formal or informal *'ties'* could complement the in-house R&D capacity of a firm (Freeman, 1991). The formal network between the firms joint research, joint development are the examples of corporate networks. Various empirical studies of the relationship between the network and innovation mainly focuses on formal ties. Researchers focused on high-technology industries and patents as proxy indicators. This stream of research documents that there is a strong and positive correlation between the alliance formation and innovation process among various industries. Many large firms joined various forms of research alliances to take advantages of information shearing. The company has more opportunity to find out what is going on in the latest technology development. It can take part in various R&D project conducted by other parties. It can even encourage other parties to develop technically in such a way so that it fulfills its own interest (Hakansson, 1989). Thus, by joining a network corporate enterprise can be benefited by cost shearing, acquiring technical expertise, pilot plant or prototype development. These kinds of collaborations thought to be evolved as a means to avert market failure, for the smaller firms where cost of R&D is too high. The crucial point here is that the most strategic and sensitive R&D information in large firms remains to be in-house for competitive reasons. By joining research, collaboration corporate complements their R&D capability rather than substitute their indigenous innovation capability (Freeman, 1991).

Network alliances among the firms irrespective of their size either large or small may involve a particular type of network or more than one kind of network. Freeman viewed networking arrangement of firms as a temporary trend of adaptation and diffusion of new and generic technologies. As the firms become more and more familiar with the technology, it will shift from the cooperative arrangement and finally they will keep strategically sensitive areas under their direct control. Hence, he anticipated that new wave of rationalization and industrial reorientation will be the trend in high technology firms particularly the ICT and pharmaceutical firms.

Strategic alliance by any firm is "...*any voluntarily initiated cooperative agreement between firms that involves exchange, sharing, or co-development, and it can include contributions by partners of capital, technology, or firm-specific asset*s" (Gulati 1999, 1998). Depends upon the degree of inter-organizational interdependency and levels of internalization Narula & Duysters (2004) categorize R&D alliance into *Equity* and *Non-Equity arrangements*. In equity alliance, the wholly owned subsidiary is the extreme form where the newly emerged subsidiary depends with the parent. Where as in Arm's length is where the participating firms remain completely independent of each other. Equity-based agreements represent a higher level of internalization and inter-organizational interdependence than no equity agreements (Narula & Duysters 2004). However, joint ventures in developing country sometimes may not be considered as equity cooperative arrangements or alliances because of government restrictions (Narula & Duyester 2004). Sometimes host-country government-imposed restrictions on the ownership of domestic companies by foreign investors. So, sometimes many joint ventures were only undertaken to abide host country government rules Although, the traditional joint ventures were generally undertaken across several activities, like marketing and production. The latest trends in joint ventures are formed primarily to conduct R&D are often referred to as research corporations.

Several key concepts of networks provide potent analytical tools that apply across different types of networks and permit assessment of their effects. Between two network partner tie is "Strong tie" if the interaction is on regular basis (Granovetter, 1973). Weak tie is a small time acquaintance and friends of friends. However, much information is available from weak tie in the form of novelty in different ideas. *Structural hole* is the potential connection between clusters of units that are not connected. The potentiality of making such connection provides advantage, or opportunity for potential and future investment. The three aspects of network structure paly different role in innovation process. Direct tie serves as source of resources and information, indirect tie serves as source of information and structure holes between two partners plays two contradictory roles. Although, structural holes expand the horizon of firms in terms of diversity of information sources but on the other hand exposes firms for other wrongful conduct (Ahuja, 2000).

There is a debate in network analysis as whether strong ties, bridge or structural wholes offer greater opportunity for innovation. Strong ties between two parties may restrict information gathering in terms of breath of search but the information that is exchanged is thick, detailed, or rich. Weak ties are thinner and less durable but provide better access to non-redundant information.

Summary

Globalization of R&D was mainly restricted to triad countries (North America, Europe and Japan). MNEs usually set up their R&D centers away from their home base to the foreign locations of other developed countries to enhance their R&D capability in home or to meet the host countries' local market demand. However, in recent years, there is a significant shift in this trend. Globally MNEs are R&D outsourcing their R&D to the developing countries in global south particularly in India and China. This new phenomenon has become a subject of interest among the research scholars and policy makers from both developing and developed countries. The developed countries are worried about the possible hollowing up of National Innovation capabilities due to increasing offshoring of R&D into the developing country. Developing host countries are concerned about the possible benefits from the MNE's R&D centres. Although, there are many different models of foreign R&D and its possible implication from host countries respective. Limited research works has been carried out from developing countries' perspective. Hence, a new typology of foreign R&D and its various aspects requires in-depth investigation.

CHAPTER III. RESEARCH ON FOREIGN R&D IN INDIA AND CHINA

Introduction

Earlier chapter reviews the research works on Globalization of R&D and its various aspects including the motivation, cost and benefit, Linkage and knowledge spill over under the broader analytical framework. This chapter reviews the scholarly publications of foreign R&D literature on both China and India. This chapter chronologically reviews the evolution of Scholarly research on the topic. The genesis of Multinational (MNEs) firms R&D in China and India happened after the economic liberalization in India in the year 1991 and in China in 1981.

Earlier, Indian government's development strategy was constructed on very strict control over private sector. Chinese industry centered on import substitution, public sector dominance and centrally planned economics. However, the scenario changed since late 1990's. The policy and decision makers of India and China adopted new development strategies. China brought a paradigm shift in national economy and liberalized their economy. India started deregulating its economy since mid-1980. The broad characteristic of the change was the liberalized national economy, less government regulations, bigger roles of private sectors and finally the integration with the global economy (Siddharthan & Narayanan, 2010).

Foreign R&D in India

India has witnessed a major surge in FDI from $129 million in 1991-92 to $150 billion in 2020. The FDI inflow has increased even in the time of global Covid-19 pandemic. The FDI to India increased because Indian government have opened up its economy gradually with FDI- favorable policies. However, many sectors like retail, defense, and print media are still lagging behind in FDI because of government's restriction of FDI in these sectors (Nagpal, 2010).

Since the last couple of decades, India is gradually becoming a favorable destination for IT and business process outsourcing (BPO). Now, it is emerging as a major center for cutting-edge R&D projects for global multinationals. Firms has the advantage of high skilled and low-cost work force. India is continuing as a favorable destination for the MNEs since 1985, when Texas Instruments first set up R&D center in Bangalore (Satyanand, 2007). The firms may enter into Indian market as wholly owned subsidiary or other form of R&D alliances like contract research and so on (Balakrishna & Balakrishna, 2003). The R&D projects are for Indian market and for high-end product generation for global market. For example, Motorola has R&D centre in India produce a low-cost mobile phone for emerging markets. Intel has thousands of India-based high skilled engineers presently working on software and hardware designs for its communication and semiconductor products. Other US based MNEs are designing everything from auto parts to consumer electronics in India through subcontracting, outsourcing or setting up their own manufacturing facilities. Firms are concentrated the cities such as in Bangalore, popularly known as India's Silicon Valley, Hyderabad, Delhi (Knowledge@Wharton, 2005). Foreign MNEs R&D investments in India are mainly concentrated on information and communication technology, telecommunications, automotive, pharmaceutical sectors. In terms of the nationality European, South Korean companies, and US prefer to invest India (Asakawa & Som, 2008).

However, different empirical evidences indicate that foreign R&D in China and India is still limited in sectoral and regional scope (Bruche, 2009). Further, Bruche (2009) argues that the investment is initially more towards *market seeking* in China (because China is a huge market of 1.3 billion customers) and more *resource seeking* in India (as India has a huge reservoir of low cost high skilled workers). However, there is a clear inclination towards evolutionary learning-based upgrading in both countries. In addition, there is a clear indication that, knowledge integration and appropriation remain hierarchical and still deeply rooted in the triad region. With the historical shift in the global loci of innovation and power there is a growing concern predominantly from the US, of the potential loss or hollowing out of national innovation capacity is found to be exaggerated (Bruche 2009).

Scholarly Research on foreign R&D in India

As discussed above, foreign R&D investment in India is increasing. However, academic research in this field has not kept pace as expected (Asakawa & Som, 2008). Although, there is abundant scholarly literature available on the subject in international context, the opportunities and challenges of managing R&D is different in these countries from those in the developed countries in Europe and America. Because of the different socioeconomic and demographic conditions of both the countries are quite different. Therefore, dealing with this phenomenon from the perspective of these countries' context, a separate stream of literature is required.

Technology Information Forecasting and Assessment Council (TIFAC), Government of India conducted a survey of foreign R&D MNEs published in 2005 (study period 1998-2003). The TIFAC survey is the first comprehensive survey of foreign R&D investment in India. (TIFAC 2005). According to the TIFAC report over 100 foreign MNCs have opened R&D centers in India over the last decade. This trend is continuing and more and more firms are entering and announcing their

R&D investment in India. In terms of their R&D activity, some of them are involved in incremental innovations to support the local market need and few of them developing new products for global market. There are also variations in their R&D activity. For example, earlier, many MNEs R&D units were to support their local production unit, later many of them opened dedicated R&D centres to meet the need for global market. Although, it is premature to access the outcome of increasing foreign R&D investment by MNEs in India but there must have some positive impact on Indian National Innovation System. However, it depends on the ability, preparedness and host country's policy (Mrinalini & Wakdikar 2008, Mrinalini 2009).

Indian economy was opened in 1991 with the tread liberalisation. However, India did not allow firms to do R&D in India. With the decline of R&D in public funding for research in 1990s, also lack of investment of Indian companies in R&D, the government of India decided to encourage foreign multinationals to invest in R&D to stimulate the research base in the country. Therefore, with the economic liberalization, India ease restrictions on MNEs to set up research and development (R&D) centres. However, India put exception of research in "atomic energy and related matters". These areas are put out of foreign firms' reach to do R&D in India. This led to foreign MNEs to establish R&D centres in in almost all areas of science and engineering. Indian government allowed, foreign participation in a wide range of industries including, including information and communication industries, electronics, marine engineering, aeronautics engineering and so on. Moreover, government also allowed MNEs to be majority equity holders in facilities for technical testing and analysis (Jayaraman, 1994).

Reddy (1997) have observed that since the mid-1980s, MNEs have started their R&D operations in developing countries. He further identified that the driving forces behind of foreign R&D were technology-related and cost-related (Reddy, 1997). Firms are establishing their linkages between the local innovation systems and firm's global R&D network. These types of alliance with foreign firms help developing countries into the global technology development activities (Reddy, 1997). Reddy & Sigurdson (1997) found that the primary driving forces behind the firms' motive to open R&D centres in India was to gain access to scientific workers as well as to reduce R&D costs. This phenomenon was mainly observed in science-based technologies mainly to find talent worldwide. The study further investigated the integration of R&D and manufacturing activities across different cultural settings, and the firms to deal with the problems such as inadequate patent laws (Reddy & Sigurdson, 1997).

Mrinalini & Wakdikar (2008) have observed that this recent phenomenon of firms' setting up R&D in India was due to the resource shortage in developed countries. This happens due to the increasing demand on S&T infrastructure in one hand and the high cost of skilled workers in the developed countries. These two pushes and pull factors are the major motives of firms to set up R&D centres in India. Moreover, high skilled workers and the reasonably developed S&T infrastructure in India is the major motives of firms to come to India to establish R&D centres. Presence of foreign R&D have some positive spill over in Indian innovation system. To get the benefits foreign R&D Government conducive policy package is utmost required for maximizing the benefits (Mrinalini & Wakdikar, 2008).

During the early to mid-1990s, foreign R&D activities were mainly restricted to 'one way technology transfer' or 'adaptive R&D' rather than 'creative R&D'. However, a paradigm shift was observed in early 2000's and India become an important destination and transform from 'one way' to two-way knowledge transfer. Many foreign R&D units are developing products from India for their global product mandate by linking with the global production networks (Krishna, Patra, & Bhattacharya, 2012).

The sector wise R&D initiatives of MNEs in India observed that FDI inflow for R&D is insignificant in comparison to the total FDI flows in India. Foreign firms patent from India do not reflect their R&D activities. Sector wise investment showed that major part of the FDI in R&D was is invested in ICT sector (Mrinalini, Nath & Sandhya, 2013).

MNEs are going to emerging markets for sourcing knowledge from globally dispersed knowledge hubs. MNEs enter Indian market not only for potential markets and 'cheap' skilled human resources but also for knowledge hubs dispersed in different cities in India. Foreign R & D centers have developed linkages with the local actors in the innovation systems in India. Most of the foreign firms are collaborating with the other foreign firms located in India. Moreover, Indian firms are preferable partners compared to university or government research institutes. Industry-academia-government linkages are quite weak in India. In terms of R&D, joint development is more prominent joint R & D. In addition, a recent trend that shows firms prefer for 'Open Innovation' mode (Patra, 2014; Patra & Krishna, 2015).

Firms' subsidiaries from the emerging markets contributes for its competitive advantage. MNEs exploit the technological and market through their subsidiaries to tap into new sources of growth. Case study of Fiat and its R&D subsidiaries in emerging markets shows that new technology creation depends on internal embeddedness (Athreye, Tuncay-Celikel, & Ujjual 2014).

Offshoring of semiconductor design to India and China has increased in recent years. It is also observed and predicted that offshoring in semiconductor design in these countries will be not displaced the design activities in the home countries of the MNEs rather it will complement the firms' capabilities in the near future (Fuller, Akinwande & Sodini, 2017).

India is an attracted location for the firms to do R&D by foreign firms. Both India and China are the favorable R&D destinations because of both 'market-driven' and 'technology-driven' factors. Foreign Firms prefer R&D locations in India and China because of qualified and highly skilled human resources available at comparatively lower cost. With these factors, MNEs' foreign-based subsidiaries are now increasingly playing a greater role in the generation, use and transmission of knowledge (Patra, 2017).

India is an attractive location for the US originated Biotech MNEs. Based on the case study based research method, it is observed that for biotech micro-Multinational Enterprises (mMNEs) from the US interested India for 'strategic asset-seeking' and 'resource-seeking motives' to start R& in India (Sooreea, Damodar, Sharma & Sooreea-Bheemul, 2018).

R&D behavior of foreign affiliates in India indicated that the firm size and the age of the firm are the major determinant of R&D of foreign firms. Further, labour intensity and outsourcing intensity are also determining factors for doing R&D by foreign firms in India (Bhat, 2020).

The evolution of Swedish MNEs' Indian R&D units shows the evolution of R&D units. The study recommended that the development of R&D competence and capability at a subsidiary cannot be solely guided by a firms headquarter and based on the local market need (Schweizer, Lagerström & Jakobsson, 2020).

Foreign R&D in China

With the opening of China's market to the outside world, many MNEs from developed countries have established manufacturing activities in China. Firms opened their operation in China to take advantage of low labour costs for manufacturing activities. The latest trend in this line is being observed that many foreign MNEs are not only established their manufacturing base in China but also have started locating their R&D activities. Firms are targeting global market from the products developed form China. Firms are talking advantages of local Chinese talent to augment their R&D strength. Since last couple of decades, Chinese government has taken various policy measures to expand and improve the country's research infrastructure. As a result, China has become a significant R&D

player on the international scene. The Chinese government is also continuously encouraging foreign investment in R&D assuming that R&D performed by MNEs in China, may be helpful to upgrade indigenous technology and skills (Lundin et.al. 2008).

However, there are many criticisms from many different corners that foreign investment may hurt China's innovative capacity. The skepticism arises due to foreign firm's conduct in China. Many of them charge high license fees for their intellectual property. In addition, presence of too many foreign firms may result, "crowd out" domestic firms. Also questions is raised about the foreign firms are controlling standards and technology platforms and reducing the role of Chinese companies to producing goods with low profit margins. Over all the latest trends of many foreign firms' R&D centre in China is a major concern for developing countries worldwide particularly in America and Europe that MNEs setting up R&D in China at the expense of Europe and the United States (Lundin et.al., 2008).

R&D by MNEs in China is a very recent occurrence. MNEs from developed countries ventured into China as a source of technology for new product development. This phenomenon is being observed since the second half of the 1990s (Boutellier at al., 2008). China's recent economic census data has confirmed that foreign R&D in China has increased significantly (Sun, 2009). According to the estimate by (Sun, 2009) thousands of foreign companies are engaged in R&D in China and employed about 150,000 R&D employees. A number of studies largely focused on foreign R&D centers/institutes in China based on ad hoc interviews or surveys. Many scholarly works on foreign R&D in China argued 'market-related' drivers are the major reason for doing R&D in China. China has a huge market of 1.3 billion customers. However, most of the R&D activities are more towards 'development' rather than 'research'. This is evidenced by the educational degree of R&D employees. Most of them are bachelor's degrees holders and only a few have doctorate degrees. This finding is substantiated by a number of scholars that foreign firms in China are doing 'adaptive R&D' to meet local customer's need (Sun et al., 2006; von Zedtwitz, 2004, Zedtwitz, 2007; Walsh, 2003; Walsh, 2007; Lundin et.al., 2008)

Scholarly Research on foreign R&D in China

China has recently become the most important investment destination for Multinational Enterprises (MNEs). Mainland China became a major destination of FDI since the mid-1990s. Deng Xiaoping visited the southern part of China in 1992. During his famous visit, he recommended the speeding up of economic reforms in the country. With the opening up of the economy, the Chinese government also encouraged inflow of FDI in various sectors. Because of this 'open door policy' central government as well as various local and provincial governments has formulated various favorable policies to attract more FDI. This increasing foreign investment (discussed in Chapter I) shows China's global position as a major market and major production site. It is assumed that the major motivations behind this growth of FDI are the Chinese market of 1.3 billion populations, and availability of cheap labor for offshore production facilities. Along with the significant inflow of FDI, MNCs are increasingly involved with local R&D activities (Gassmann & Keupp 2008). However, R&D management in China has gone largely unnoticed in the last decade of 20th century. There is very little systematic research on foreign R&D in China as this is a relatively new phenomenon. The major reason behind this may be due to difficulties in doing adequate research in China and because China-based R&D had been limited in size and impact to the outside world. Greatwall (2002) and Walsh (2003) are published a major works on foreign R&D in China. Greatwall's study was published in Chinese. Therefore, it had very limited scope to no-Chinese audience. The report published by Walsh had a strong US American biasness (Boutellier et.al. 2008).

Nortel Network established its R&D center in China in the year 1994. Nortel Networks Corporation and Beijing University of Posts and Telecommunications had jointly set up that R&D centre in Beijing. Since then MNEs, investment in R&D in China is increasing rapidly (Wen & Lin, 2005, Li & Li, 2010). This trend picked its height in 2001 when China entered into the World Trade Organization (WTO). With the China's entry in WTO, it was observed that (Prater & Jiang 2008) between November 2001 and May 2002, many MNEs have opened R&D center or announced substantial raise in investment or workers. However, scholarly works and popular medium like press releases by firms and newspaper reports time to time highlighted that many of the 'fortune 500' firms have opened their R&D centres in, major cities like Beijing, Shanghai and so on (Motohashi 2005). With this trends China has advanced from *"design it abroad, make it in China, sell it in abroad"* cycle to globally recognized R&D major (Prater & Jiang 2008). This has been confirmed from various press announcements (People's Daily, International Trade Daily, and China Daily). More R&D investment trend is being observed particularly in the ICT industries, because both these industries are highly dependent on skilled R&D workers and, has fast production cycles (Walsh, 2003). For example, Microsoft established its first Asia Research Institute (its second overseas base) in Beijing, in 1998. By 2010, Microsoft doubled its R&D employees up to 3,000 and about 1,500 project-based researchers in China. Motorola has about 25 R&D centers in China and the firm has invested about 500 million dollars on the R&D (Li & Li, 2010). Beside the ICT industry, major investment in R&D also are from chemical, petrochemical, bio technology, pharmaceutical, automotive, transportation and power generation equipments. Although, there is a significant amount of investment in R&D from Hong Kong and Taiwan, however, majority of MNEs are from developed countries, particularly from triad regions (Gassmann & Han 2004). Above all, foreign R&D has become a significant phenomenon in China. Thousands of foreign companies are engaged in R&D in China and according to Sun (2009), foreign R&D centers generates about 150,000 high skilled jobs in China. Regarding the activity foreign firms of foreign firms, few scholars argue that most of them are adaptive R&D and more towards the development than research. This argument is supported by the fact that most of the R&D employees from these foreign R&D centres are bachelor degree holder and very few of them have doctoral degrees (Walsh, 2003, von Zedtwitz, 2004; Sun et al., 2006; Sun, 2009).

The scholarly research onMNEs' R&D activities in China mostly concentrate on the description of the current situation, the reasons for MNEs' R&D investment in China and local factors that affect MNEs' investment decisions and on the benefits and challenges arising from MNEs' R&D activities in China. To map the R&D activities in China, Lundin et al (2008) did a research project using a questionnaire survey and interviews in Beijing and Shanghai. These two cities are the major locations of MNEs' R&D centres in China. This research conducted Tsinghua University's research team in 2004-2006 gave a further understanding of MNEs' strategy and activities (Lundin et al 2008).

Xue & Liang (2005) found that low R&D costs are the main motive for MNEs to establish R&D centre in China. Also, because of gradual rising wages in Beijing and Shanghai, many companies are considering setting up other R&D branches in "Tire II cities" or "second-line cities," such as Nanjing, Xi'an, and Chengdu. The study also found that the foreign R&D centers in China is a mix of both "knowledge exploiting" and "knowledge exploring" categories. Perhaps one major finding is that foreign R&D centers mainly interact with their own networks and little or no collaborations with different national actors of innovation system. However, foreign firms' linkages with Chinese universities or research institutes, are deeper as seen from joint research centers and other forms of collaborations. (Xue & Liang 2005).

Asakawa & Som (2008) observed that the growing trend of foreign R&D investment in China and India. However, academic research in this field is not adequate. However, there is an increasing stream of literature is emerging. They suggested the MNEs unique challenges and capabilities in China and India (Asakawa & Som 2008).

MNEs have heavily invest in China in recent years. With the increasing investment in manufacturing and other activities, research and development (R&D) have also increased rapidly. Wen & Lin 2005 has observed using quantitative interviews method with R&D managers of foreign R&D in China that with the increase investment there was a strategic change of MNEs R&D strategies in China. The R&D strategies changed from cooperation alliance with the local firms to foreign-owned R&D institutes. They further observed that it changed from "Development" to "Research and Development" (Wen & Lin, 2005).

Von Zedtwitz, M. (2004) investigated the management of foreign R&D units. Based on R&D directors and managers of foreign R&D units in Chia, conducted between 2001 and 2004 observed that foreign R&D laboratories in China are working for not only technology for local market development but also increasingly developing technology for global market (Von Zedtwitz, 2004).

With the growth of Chinese economy in recent years, there is an increase in foreign R&D activities in China. MNEs Chinese R&D units are characterized by decentralized R&D activities (Gassmann & Han, 2004).

Shanghai has become one of the most concentrated centers of foreign R&D in China. Shanghai is attractive location for quality labour at the local scale. Sun, Du, & Huang (2006) have observed that most of the foreign R&D in China is of 'adaptive type'. Firms generally conduct these types of R&D to meet the need of local Chinese market. However, a few firms also conduct strategic R&D only for China's local markets, but also for the global market. Few firms also do both short-term product development, and long-term original research (Sun, Du, & Huang, 2006).

With the increasing presence and investment of R&D by MNEs in Shanghai, a stream of literature evolved to study the impact the characteristics, problems, incentives and reasons of R&D investment of MNEs in Shanghai (Xie, 2006). A case study of Lucent China Research and Technology Center found the effective cultural adjustment with the R&D project management has gained remarkable success in quality improvement and productivity enhancement (Xie, 2006).

Von Zedtwitz et. al., (2007) have observed that although, China is one of the favorable destinations to do R&D, intellectual property protection in China was weak. They were quite skeptical about the nature and dynamics of foreign R&D in China. They further suggest that China-based R&D must be part of a firm's China strategy and must be the part of firms global R&D (Von Zedtwitz, Ikeda, Gong, Carpenter, & Hämäläinen 2007).

Sun & Wen (2007) examined the challenges of foreign R&D) in China. They found three major types of barriers. These include institutional environment, infrastructure and labor management. Labor management includes the increasing cost and mobility, experience, creativity and cultural differences among the research staff (Sun & Wen 2007).

Sun & Wen (2007) examined the location of foreign R&D in China. The study found that firms R&D facilities mainly concentrated in Shanghai and Beijing. They found that the degree of concentration was not only based on the factors such as market size, labor costs and infrastructure but also because of imitative behaviors along with the factors such as uncertainties and multiple risks. The study further suggested attracting R&D in locations other than the Tire I cities like Beijing and Shanghai. MNEs will begin to establish R&D facilities in such second-tier cities with cultural proximity (Sun & Wen, 2007).

Sun, Von Zedtwitz, & Simon, (2007) discuss the MNEs R&D strategies in China. They observed that overseas R&D by

MNEs had increased. Foreign R&D had a major shift from the adaptive R&D to more critical and strategic global R&D. China had become one major attraction for foreign R&D due to low-cost but skilled scientists and engineer. The foreign R&D investment is also related to the rapid growth of China's domestic investment in R&D. The study further raised the concern the value China can incur from the presence of foreign R&D centers (Sun, Von Zedtwitz & Simon, 2007).

Gassmann & Keupp (2008) observed that during the first decade of 21st century among 400 out of the Fortune Top 500 have established at least one R&D unit in China. They found that these R&D activities contradict existing theory on international R&D. They propose that firms conduct foreign R&D to acquire competitive advantage (Gassmann & Keupp, 2008).

Japanese companies' FDI in China have concentrated mainly in manufacturing sector. The motives and strategies of Japanese firms R&D labs in China are driven by both 'technology push' and 'demand pull' strategies (Miyazaki & Ying, 2009).

Foreign companies have started significant R&D activities in China. Jolly & Masetti-Placci (2016) investigated the location, people and intellectual property rights, and relationships with Chinese authorities. The study observed the foreign R&D China operate in a different environment. However, the Chinese research, development and innovation landscape has evolved rapidly. China has occupied prominent position in terms scientific publications and patent the firms. Foreign firms can exploit the Chinese strength in R&D (Jolly & Masetti-Placci, 2016).

Holmes, Li, Hitt, DeGhetto & Sutton (2016) examined various factors of motivating and demotivating foreign firms to start R&D in China. These include location advantages (e.g., economic growth) and disadvantages (e.g., weak intellectual property protection). Both the factors have both independent and joint effects on MNEs' establishment of China R&D centers (Holmes, Li, Hitt, DeGhetto & Sutton, 2016).

Liu, Guo, Lei, & Feng, (2018) have studied the impact of foreign R&D in Chinese innovation ecosystem. They observed that foreign R&D in Chinese innovation ecosystem. The region wise analysis showed that there is variation in the structure (Liu, Guo, Lei, & Feng, 2018).

von Zedtwitz, Ikeda, Gong, Carpenter, & Hämäläinen, (2018) raised the concern about Chinese innovation and weak intellectual property protection. They further suggest that foreign firms must adopt Chinese R&D in their global strategy. This can avoid various pitfalls of managing R&D in China (von Zedtwitz, Ikeda, Gong, Carpenter, & Hämäläinen, 2018) because the motivation of US firms to open R&D units in China is derived mostly match those found in more developed countries (Chiarini, Caliari, Bittencourt, & Siqueira Rapini 2020).

Yang, Matsuura, & Ito (2019) investigated R&D and patenting activities of foreign firms in China. The study observed that local market-oriented firms do more R&D than process export-oriented firms. Moreover, local market-oriented firms filed more patents to protect their products in the domestic market. Hence, their patenting activities are comparative to the scientific firms (Yang, Matsuura & Ito 2019).

Summary

This chapter deals with the review of scholarly literature of foreign R&D in India and China by Multinational enterprises. The chapter extensively reviewed global literature on the subject. It is evident from the literature review that the subject is getting attention from the scholars worldwide, However, Chinese case is more focused and getting more attention than the Indian case. Moreover, there is a gap in understanding the actual nature and dynamics of R&D by MNEs in these two-emerging economics. The chapter follows will deal with the selected firms and their R&D activities in India and China to further understanding the issue and add value to the existing knowledge.

CHAPTER IV. MOTIVATION OF FOREIGN R&D BY FIRMS IN INDIA AND CHINA

Introduction

The theory of the MNEs contends that technological innovation in home or abroad is the main source of a firm's competitive advantage. However, empirical evidences show that major reason for dispersion of MNEs is to secure new technological competencies that are dispersed globally. A firm's global growth can be considered as a result of home based 'ownership advantages' and 'competitive advantage' for exploitation in the foreign markets. However, present day internationalization approaches of firms are radically different from the earlier international strategy of mid-20th century. A major shift has been taken place and new mode of organizing transnational corporations' innovative activities has gradually emerged. As discussed in Chapter II various scholarly works show that, the main aim of MNEs was to explore new markets through the adaptation of products developed in local market according to the local customer's need. Also, during that period MNEs also started establishing networks of subsidiaries to transfer technology, skills and assets across national borders between the head quarter and subsidiaries. Local R&D units are also becoming increasingly important for acquiring new knowledge from the local environment for the parent unit at home base (Cantwell & Piscitello, 2005). Thus, it is two-way interaction process between a firm's headquarter and its subsidiary. Zanfei (2000) identified that, MNE's foreign-based subsidiaries, are increasingly playing a greater role in the generation, use and transmission of knowledge. Also, MNEs are developing external networks of relationships with local counterparts, through which foreign affiliates acquire external knowledge (Zanfei 2000).

Usually, among many other corporate functions, offshore R&D by multinationals is usually considered to be the one of the last corporate functions to internationalize in the value chain (Mansfield, 1979). However, till the end of last century, internationalization of R&D was distributed on a triad region (the 'triad' being the US, Western Europe, and Japan). The internationalization of R&D was a regional phenomenon rather than a true 'global' phenomenon (Rugman & Verbeke 2003). Rugman & Verbeke (2003) provided empirical evidence that demonstrates that the majority of even the most 'global' MNEs in reality concentrated on regional/triad basis. According to that study, about 20 globally dispersed MNEs; only a few firms have adopted true global strategies. Most of them were restricted in the triad regions.

However, UNCTAD report of 2005 observed that there was a major shift from that. The first half of the 21st century showed a new form of 'Asian dynamism'. China becomes the second largest economy in the world after the US. In addition, India is going to take the third largest economy by 2035 (Kaplinsky & Messner, 2008). As a result, there is growing interest among MNEs around the world to exploit these two major and emerging Asian giant's markets. Moreover, China and India have become specialized hubs in global value chains, because of the knowledge-intensive goods and services. These countries are increasingly moving up along the global value chain (Chaminadea & Vang, 2008).

Motivations to set up foreign R&D

Innovation has significant consequences for a firm's economic performance. However, all firms cannot earn benefits from the innovation. Firms need to have a sufficient level of internationalization to progress through innovation. Firms cannot earn benefit from innovation if their international activities are below a threshold level (Kafouros et. al, 2008). Although, MNE performs most of their R&D activity in the home country a number of recent studies have found that foreign R&D by MNEs are increasing to exploit benefit from foreign R&D. Drawing upon Boddewyn's (1985) work, Cheng & Bolon (1993) classified three important factors responsible for increasing MNEs R&D activities. These factors are *conditions*, *motivations*, and *precipitating circumstances*.

The motives behind FDI in R&D are combinations of various push and pull factors. The motives can be broadly categories into three types. These are *market seeking, resource seeking and efficiency-seeking* (Lundvall, 2008; UNCTAD, 2007). However, some other factors such as host country's business environment, intellectual property right protections are also important. According to von Zedtwitz & Gassmann (2002) firms generally concentrated their research activities only in a few concentrated pockets worldwide. However, their developmental activities are globally dispersed (von Zedtwitz & Gassmann, 2002). In that view, the geographical location of R&D by MNEs can be analyzed in terms of two competing and contradictory forces i.e. 'Centrifugal forces' (decentralization) and 'Centripetal forces' (centralization) (Chiesa, 1996).

Several empirical surveys and case studies have observed various factors of motivation and determinants of decentralization of R&D. For example, during the second half of 1980's Japanese firms were actively engaged in overseas R&D activity to support their local market needs (Odagiri & Yasuda 1996). Later the trend among the Japanese MNEs R&D activities abroad showed that the basic and applied research of overseas subsidiaries targeted at the exploitation of foreign advanced technological knowledge. However, the host country's market size was the determining factor for development and design activities (Shimizutani & Todo 2008). The survey by Thrusby & Thrusby (2006) analyzed the factors that influence the decisions of the location of R&D. They found that the following major motivating factors; market potential, R&D personnel, collaboration with the universities, and intellectual property protection. While in setting up R&D units in developing countries, the most important influencing factor the firm first considered was the market size. It was followed by the quality of R&D personnel. Tax incentives by various host country governments, the expertise of university faculty was also among the important motivating factors. However, MNEs were concerned about the host country's intellectual property protection. Study of German and Non-German MNEs operating in Germany showed that the market adaptation of products was still the major driver for German MNEs, but international knowledge seeking was increasingly important, especially in technological areas that were linked very closely to the basic research. Germany as a host of international industrial R&D was much more attractive location for applied research (mechanical engineering) than for basic research (Edler 2004). The determinants of the foreign R&D location MNEs showed that most of the cases (nearly 70 percent) MNEs locate their activities abroad in technological areas or fields where they were strong at home. However, it differed depend upon the MNEs country of origin. For Example, the strategy of Japanese firms was very different from European and US MNEs. Japanese firms pursued for the locations that have complementary strengths to their own (Le Bas & Sierra 2002). Although there are a number of studies that identified various motives for motives internationalizing R&D. One of them by Gammeltoft (2006) who divided the motives into six categories: *market-driven*, *production-driven*, *technology-driven*, *innovation-driven*, *cost-driven* and *policy-driven* (Gammeltoft, 2006).

Motivations to Set up R&D in India

Texas Instruments Incorporated, an American technology company set up its R&D centre in Bangalore, India in 1985. This is the first MNEs that started its operation in R&D in India. After that, many more foreign firms have started their R&D centres in India. After that many MNEs in almost every sector have started their R&D activities in India (Balakrishna & Balakrishna Aug 06, 2003). The motivations for the firms to start R&D operations in India can be categorized under the following broad headings:

Firstly, The High skilled manpower is the major motive of firms to come in India. Although, there are several driving factors for foreign firms to set up R&D centers in India. Among the many other reasons, availability of the high skilled work force at low cost is the major factor. India has a huge pool of high quality, technically qualified and English-speaking work force. Therefore, the availability of high skilled workers is the possible reason for the establishment of R&D centres in India (Reddy, 1997).

Secondly, the low costs of R&D operation are perhaps is the second most important factor. Indian R&D operation costs one-fifth of developed countries like US or Europe. Various newspaper articles and press briefing reported that companies shifted their R&D to India because it reduced substantial amount of cost in their operation (Sharma, Chakki & Varmani, 2020).

Thirdly, India has developed a good infrastructure of universities, government research centres and national research laboratories. Today India has more than 1000 public and private universities. India has government sponsored laboratories for example Department of Biotechnology, Council of Scientific and Industrial Research. These institutes are excellent entities to collaborate. Firms can collaborate for R&D with these institutes

Finally, Indian government encourage foreign companies to establish R&D centres. Foreign firm's approvals are quite easy Now. Indian government encourage firms open their business from every sectors particularly in software industry situated in Software Technology Park (STP). Firms can get tax breaks and other facilities including duty free imports.

Motivation of firms to set up R&D units in India – selected cases

Keeping all the above-mentioned factors, the following section will present the motivation of firms to establish R&D units in India taking examples from the press statement, news briefs and newspaper reports from various sources.

Market

Market is a major motive for firms to start their R&D operation in India. The following statements of firms extracted from various newspaper reports, news briefings and press statements show that Indian market is major motive for firms.

Cisco Systems, Inc. has a large engineering team based in India. It has more than 10,000 R&D and technical staff in its various facilities. In an interview in 2020, Cisco President of Asia Pacific, Japan and Greater China (APJC), Miyuki Suzuki told,

> India and Cisco have a very symbiotic relationship, where we drive good business yet very high growth rates. India was the highest growing theatre for me in the APJC region during the last fiscal year"(PTI, 2020).

According to ETTelecom report, Nokia Corporation's business grew by more than 10% in the year 2020. The firm wants to acquire over 25 percent market share and at the top position in India's optical network market (ET Telecom, 2021).

Human resources

As discussed earlier that India has abundant supply of high skilled low-cost work force. India has a good infrastructure of government research laboratories. India has also world class educational institute. There are about 1200 universities impart quality education in the country. Looking at this huge potential of English-speaking quality researchers, International Business Machines Corporation (IBM), the American MNE intended to set up an artificial intelligence (AI) Centre of Excellence (CoE) unit in partnership with the Government e-Marketplace (GeM). According to Arvind Krishna the CEO of the company

> AI is one of the biggest technology revolutions of our time and I am convinced that India is uniquely positioned to lead (IBM to set up centre of excellence for AI with government e-marketplace, 2020).

Microsoft Corporation an American software MNE has opened a new India Development Centre (IDC) in India. This newly established R&D centre located in Noida, near New Delhi. It is one of its largest R&D centers of the company outside of their Redmond headquarter in the US (FE Online, 2021). In a press statement the firm said,

> The centre will build on Microsoft's commitment to tap India's world-class engineering talent to create solutions for global impact," Microsoft IDC "… will play a critical role in Microsoft India's expansion and growth story. The facility will open opportunities for thousands of engineers, with plans to expand to a full-fledged development centre, similar to IDC facilities in Bengaluru and Hyderabad (PTI, 2020).

Global Market Product

Cisco Systems, Inc, the American MNE from semiconductor industry has significant R&D operation in India. Mr. Sanjay Kaul the Managing Director, Service Provider Business, Cisco India & SAARC region said in an interview to the Financial Express,

> We have a huge R&D centre here. Our focus on R&D has improved like never before…. Today, we are not only building for India but we are building solutions and services for the global market from India. Some of the large numbers

of routers deployment that we had in India, their software and hardware development had happened locally (Mohd, U, 2018).

Hewlett Packard Enterprise (HPE) India observed a significant growth of their business from India. Mr. Som Satsangi, Managing Director HPE told The Economic times,

> …its R&D labs in Bengaluru have been adding significant value globally and working on almost all development for software and infrastructure services. For instance, majority of the backend technology work for HPE Info-Sight tool, which enables data centres to deliver hybrid cloud environment, is done in these labs (Pramanik, 2019).

Local customer demand

Motorola, Inc an American MNE from telecommunication industry considers India as an important market for the company. Accordingly, the company launch products specific to local Indian market. Magnus Ahlqvist, the corporate vice president of Motorola, said in an interview to the DNA,

> India is one of the most important markets for us, not only because of its sheer size and value proposition, but it is also the only market in the world where we decided to launch only via e-commerce and with just one partner – making it very significant in terms of internal visibility, and this has inspired us to use this strategy in other markets as well (Beryl M, 2014).

General expansion/Strategic decision

A couple of firms generally started their R&D operation as their general strategy of expansion in global market including India. For example, Telefonaktiebolaget LM Ericsson, a Swedish MNE in networking and telecommunications industry observed a good growth in radio access network (RAN) hardware sales in the year 2020 (IANS, 2021). The company announced the setting up of a Global Artificial Intelligence Accelerator (GAIA) in Bengaluru, India to do R&D on Artificial Intelligence and automation. The firms said that their Bengaluru centre will work in coordination with US and Sweden R&D centre on AI and automation. The company think that GAIA will use Indian rich talent pool as well as the vibrant ecosystem (Chowdhary, 2018).

Foreign R&D in China

Mainland China is now a major destination of FDI. As seen from the flow of FDI into China, the country is a FDI attractor since the mid-1990s. Deng Xiaoping during his famous 'southern visit in 1992' recommended the speeding up of economic reform and encourages inflow of FDI from all over the world. Because of his 'open door policy' central government as well as various local and provincial governments has formulated various favorable policy measures to attract more inward FDI in China.

According to a news report of China Daily published in 2006, the Ministry of Commerce, People's Republic of China estimated that about 750 foreign-funded R&D centres have been set up in China. President Hu Jintao told that *"China encourages multinationals to establish R&D centres in China,"*. These R&D centres were mainly located in large cities for example in Beijing, Shanghai and Shenzhen and so on. In terms of sector wise break up most of the foreign-funded R&D centres in China were in the fields of electronic and telecommunications equipment manufacturing, transport equipment manufacturing, medicine production and chemical industry. Although most foreign-funded R&D centres were focused on application technology, some such as Microsoft, Nokia, Bell-Alcatel and Panasonic also conduct basic R&D research (Foreign firms hasten R&D establishment in mainland, 2006).

With the opening of China's market to the outside world, many MNEs from developed countries established manufacturing activities in China to take advantage of low labor costs for manufacturing operations. The latest trend is being observed that even many foreign MNEs have started their R&D

operation in China. Those firms target global market form China R&D centres taking advantage of local Chinese talent.

Since last couple of decades, Chinese government, has taken various policy measures to expand and improve the country's research infrastructure. Therefore, China is now a major R&D destination. The Chinese government is also continuously encouraging foreign investment in R&D assuming that R&D performed by MNEs in China, will be helpful for the advancement of indigenous technology and skills (Lundin et.al. 2008).

However, there are many criticisms from many different corners that too much foreign investment may hurt China's innovative capacity. The skepticism arises due to foreign firm's conduct in China. Many of them charge high license fees for their intellectual property. Also, presence of too many foreign firms may result, "crowd out" domestic firms. It is a matter of concern both from within China as well as globally. Chinese concern is on the Chinese companies and their low profit margins. American and European concern is on the hollowing effect. They are concerned that MNEs setting up R&D in China at the expense of Europe and the United States (Lundin et.al., 2008).

The reasons for MNEs' R&D investment in China and local factors that affect MNEs' investment decisions and on the benefits and challenges arising from MNEs' R&D activities in China. To map the R&D activities in China, Lundin et al (2008) did a research project using a questionnaire survey and interviews in Beijing and Shanghai, the two major locations of MNEs' R&D centres in China, by Tsinghua University research team in 2004-2006. The study gave a further understanding of MNEs' strategy and activities (Lundin et al., 2008).

Xue & Liang (2005) found that low R&D costs are the main motive for MNEs to establish R&D centre in China. In addition, because of gradual rising wages in Beijing and Shanghai, many companies are considering setting up other R&D branches in "Tire II cities" or "second-line cities," such as

Nanjing, Xi'an, and Chengdu. The study also found that the foreign R&D centres in China is a mix of both "knowledge exploiting" and "knowledge exploring" categories. Perhaps one major finding is that foreign R&D centers mainly interact with their own networks and little or no collaborations with different national actors of innovation system. However, foreign firms' linkages with Chinese universities or research institutes are deeper as seen from joint research centers and other forms of collaborations. (Xue & Liang 2005).

Motivations to set up R&D in China

Deng Xiaoping's open-door policy in 1992 accelerated FDI in China. Chinese government also encouraged local government to attract FDI in provincial level. The Inward FDI in China was about US$149.32 bn in 2020.

According to Motohashi (2010) major motivation of firms behind FDI are the *cheap labor* for offshore production. In addition, China is a big market of 1.3 billion customers. Along with the FDI in manufacturing foreign firms also invested in R&D activity. Among the many reasons of investment in R&D might be the production support, product localization to home market, local consumers' needs. Motohashi (2010) further observed that, scientific research at Chinese universities has improved, because of government's initiatives to promote S&T and high-technology developments. Therefore, many foreign firms are increasingly collaborating with the Chinese universities at different levels. China has also highly qualified S&T work force. This vast pool of human resources allows multinationals to tap vast Chinese S&T talent at relatively lower cost (Motohashi 2010).

Although, *low cost* is the primary motivator for establishment of R&D center in China, quicker R&D cycle time is also another major motivator to respond market demand. Prater & Jiang (2008) assumed that the major driver of R&D activity has been China's entrance into the World Trade Organization (WTO). China officially joined the WTO on November 12,

2001. Further, with some case study they categorized the major motives of starting R&D center into four motives: *development of products for local Chinese market, market access strategy* by establishing linkages with government, *local talent*, product development for *global market* (Prater & Jiang 2008).

This *market driven driver* further includes factors like products customization according to the local customers' demand, new product development for the local market and to support the parent company's sales, manufacturing and other activities in Chinese market (Prater & Jiang 2008). Motohashi (2005) also found that the major motivation of foreign R&D in China was mainly of "market driven". He also found variation of foreign R&D strategy across regions. Market driven R&D was found mainly in Guangdong, which is called a world IT factory, and does not have strong universities or PRIs. Because of large number of universities and government, research institutions, foreign firms situated in Beijing and oriented more toward technology driven approach. Shanghai, with both a large industrial base as well as strong science sector, is in-between these two factors (Motohashi 2005).

China's policies in S&T development raise local firm's technological capability. In 2020, China has spent 2.44 trillion Chinese yuan ($378 billion) in R&D budget. This amount is about 10% increase from the previous year. China is continually investing in emerging technologies and in applied science areas for example biotechnology, nanotechnology. Moreover, investment also increase to build strong basic science capabilities. The benefits of these emerging technologies are spreading across different sectors. China's development of a system of peer-reviewed, merit-based competitive funding for basic research and for evaluating S&T results has the potential to stimulate more innovative and excellent research efforts at China's universities and research institutes. All these factors making China as lucrative ground for foreign MNEs to collaborate in R&D (Li & Yue 2005).

Chinese government has preferential policies to encourage foreign investments in the country. For example, foreign R&D centers are exempted certain equipment duty. Government also encourage Chinese universities and research institutes to collaborate with foreign R&D centers. These human resource advantages and investment policies have contributed to the rapid growth of international R&D investments in the country (Li & Yue 2005).

Motivation of firms to set up R&D units in China – Selected cases

This section will deal with the various motivation factors for firms to establish R& centres in China. The information has been collected from various press statement issued by firms, news reports from Chinese newspapers particularly from the China Daily. From the content analysis of news reports, the motivations are categories under the following headings.

Local Market

Intel Corporation have established its software R&D centre in China in the year 1994. The firm targeted for an initial investment of $1.3 billion and employment of about 5,000 software professionals. In the year 2005, it has established its Asia-Pacific Research and Development Ltd. (Asia-Pacific R&D Ltd.) in Shanghai, China. The firm wanted to use the growing pool of technical talents in China to augment its local R&D capabilities and also to develop and solutions for markets across Asia Pacific and even globally. Wee Theng Tan, the president of Intel China told to China Daily newspaper in an interview:

> China has one of the world's most compelling combinations of R&D talents and market potential…… As a leading technology market with a growing number of highly trained researchers and technologists, China is creating the kind of dynamic environment that is an impetus to great R&D. Intel is committed to working with the local industry to help bring

Chinese innovation into the world." (Intel Expands Research and Development In China 2005)

Motorola Inc has a long presence in China. Perhaps it was first MNEs that started its R&D center in China in the year 1993. It invested about US$3.6 billion and started 16 centres all over China and employed about 2,000 engineers. Mark Borota, one of the senior vice-president and general manager of Motorola told, "Motorola is committed to increasing local innovation in China, which will further advance China's communications market" (Li Weitao 2006).

Cisco Systems invested about $10 billion in China to gain a position in Chinese marketplace. Charles Giancarlo, chief development officer of Cisco, said that they

> ... hoped to develop the China R&D centre into "a centre of engineering excellence" and one of the top four global R&D facilities for the company in the future. The China R&D Centre will develop networking solutions for home users and small and medium-sized businesses, which are emerging as a major customer for Cisco (Li, 2005).

Hewlett-Packard celebrated its 25th anniversary in China in 2010. Isaiah Cheung, vice-president and general manager of HP told the newspaper China Daily that "...We are also considering a China innovation center to work with local governments and companies on future technologies" (HP sets sights on China's rural market 2010).

Global Market

Pfizer has many innovative products developed from its China R&D unit. It has opened its regional headquarters and clinical trial centre in Shanghai in 2003. Allan Gabor, chairman and general manager of Pfizer Pharmaceuticals Ltd China, told China Daily:

> The legal procedures for setting up the regional headquarters are now under way and the Shanghai-based clinical trial centre project is an indication of our confidence in China....

China's clinical trial centre will not only be concerned about developing drugs for local approval, but also be part of Pfizer's global R&D (research and development) network (Yan, 2003).

Customer support

Nokia invested more than 450 million yuan (US$56.3 million) and built their office in Beijing to enter into Chinese market and also the Asia-pacific market. Company Chairman and Chief Executive Officer Jorma Ollila said "...the campus would also include Nokia's research and development (R&D) centres and its existing mobile phone manufacturing base" (Li, 2006).

Ericsson launched its operation in Xi'an in 2012. Mats H Olsson, President of Ericsson of Northeast Asia Region, told,

> Global, centralized services will lead to improved efficiency and quality for our customers. The new center China site in Xi'an will allow Ericsson to expand our network-operations capabilities in China as well as our global capabilities for standardized service deliveries. (Ericsson inaugurates new global services center in Xi'an, 2012).

Moreover, Zhao Juntao, President of Ericsson China told in an interview to China Daily in October 2012 "The Xi'an facility, together with Ericsson's local service centers in Beijing, Wuhan, Guangzhou and Dalian, will offer its customers with high-quality and cost-effective services" (Ericsson inaugurates new global services center in Xi'an, 2012).

Sanofi announced the establishment of Sanofi Institute for Biomedical Research, its first global research institute in China, in Suzhou, Jiangsu in 2021. Pius S. Hornstein, country head of Sanofi China, said "The institute will help us realize the vision and become a powerful engine for us to gather local innovation efforts and R&D advantages and ultimately benefit a wider range of patients," (Zhou, 2021)

Global Strategy

Cisco Systems opened R&D centre in Shanghai in 2005. It committed and investment of US$32 million for five years. Charles Giancarlo, chief development officer of Cisco, said its R&D centre will develop into "...a centre of engineering excellence" and one of the top four global R&D facilities for the company in the future" (Li, 2015).

Talent

Cheng-Yaw Sun, president of HP China, said "China has become the most important strategic market and talent pool for HP globally... Now they are shifting the focus to the R&D activities and, most recently, are hunting for local talent" (Li, 2006)

General Expansion

In 2005, Ericsson announced for an invest $1 billion in China to expand its presence in the world's largest telecommunications market. Ericsson's Greater China president Mats Olsson said in a statement that "...the company will use the money to expand its manufacturing facilities, invest in research and development and services" (Ericsson to invest $1bln in China in 5 years, 2005).

Summary

The scholarly research on foreign R&D in India is limited. Government of India publishes a report through Technology Information Forecasting and Assessment Council (TIFAC) in the year 2005 to investigate the foreign R&D centre in China. It was the first government level estimation of foreign R&D centre in India. However, Chinese case is well researched and more highlighted than India. A number of scholars have investigated foreign R&D activity and its various aspects for example Sun et al. (2006); von Zedtwitz (2004); von Zedtwitz

(2007); Walsh (2003); Walsh (2007), Lundin et.al. (2008) to name a few.

This chapter investigates foreign R&D centers in India and China under the analytical framework of various types to motives. The motives are categorized into the following headings, local market, global market, cost, local talent and general expansion. The news from various sources for example, press statement issued by the company, news reports etc. are collected and presented. The big markets of India and China are the major motives of firms followed by the availability of R&D personal at low cost. Few firms also doing significant R&D and developing product for their global product mandate.

CHAPTER V. FIRMS AND THEIR INNOVATION POTENTIAL IN INDIA AND CHINA

Introduction

It is empirically well-established fact that MNEs are major actor in global technology development (Zander & Sölvell 2000). They are the key actors for new technology generation and development globally. Firms generally develop new technology at the home base and exploit their R&D strength generated at home in offshore location (Fors 1997). The new technology or knowledge are generally embodied in the new products, processes, proprietary technology, and business organization. So, MNEs play major role in the global production and dissemination of new productive knowledge (Caves, 2007).

Innovation is one of the major reasons for a firm to internationalize. Firms invest in R&D in offshore location to drive further profit from innovations developed at home location (Bartlett & Ghoshal 1989). In recent years empirical study observed that there is considerable increase in offshoring in R&D. This is because of firm's strategy to augment their knowledge base in both home and home country's location. FDI in R&D happens because firms exploit firm-specific capabilities (*home-base-exploiting*). To capture the global market firms, develop new products and process to extract benefits of innovations by selling or licensing its technology (Bartlett & Ghoshal, 1989). However, firms also acquire new knowledge and capabilities from different knowledge hubs dispersed globally (*home-base-augmenting*). Innovation literature has recognized the geographical "stickiness" of innovation activity. Scholarly studies have emphasized many possibilities and advantages of various innovation projects across borders and within the multinational networks (Zander & Sölvell 2000). Firms usually establish facilities close to existing manufacturing base and markets to exploit home based capabilities. Contrary to this firms usually establish facilities close to universities and other research institutions to augment home based capabilities (Kuemmerle 1999). Almeida (2002) mentioned his process of knowledge creation and transfer as the *"knowledge diffusion"* model of the MNC (Almeida, 2002).

Geographical distribution of knowledge creation is based on the fact that knowledge generation is not limited to the research labs. Technological knowledge is to some extent a public good within the MNE (Fors 1997). A firm's organizational knowledge extends beyond scientific and technical knowledge and embraces every function of the firm. Also, firm's stock of knowledge is grown not only by internal knowledge creation (learning by doing), but also through external learning. Such external learning is a potent source of value creation for MNEs. Marshall's (1920) concept of "industrial districts" and Porter's (1990) concept of localized industry "clusters" is based on the idea that industry-specific knowledge develops in geographically concentrated locations. Almeida, (2002) refer this process of knowledge generation and utilization as 'knowledge building' (Almeida, 2002).

Internationalization of R&D and its various aspects is a hotly debated issue among researchers, government and the business community. These trends observed along with the increasing trends of international generation of innovation since the early 1980s. During 1960s and 1970s, MNEs increasingly built their sales, distribution and assembly operations in foreign locations. Later, in 1970s and 1980s, MNEs shifted their R&D activity to support foreign subsidiaries' local manufacturing and other functions. The initial R&D abroad was limited to adaptation of product and process technologies from the home country based on local production and market requirements. Later, there was a clear and recognizable trend emerged, since the late 1980s. The trend was more towards strengthening the R&D in foreign countries and extending the global competence portfolio. Increasingly, research became established at a high level in foreign locations (Meyer-Krahmer & Reger 1999). The debate in several countries has revealed worries that the MNEs' exports of technology to foreign affiliates contribute to a de-industrialization or at least a hollowing out of innovation in the home country (Fors 1997). Findings from various scholarly researched suggested that MNEs were increasing their offshoring R&D outside their home country (Cheng and Bolon, 1993; Håkanson and Nobel, 1993; Meyer-Krahmer & Reger 1999). International R&D units originally been established to undertake adaptation work or because of host country demands, but gradually becoming active contributors to the MNC's global innovation effort (Bartlett & Ghoshal 1989; Pearce 1989; Papanastassiou & Pearce, 1996; Pearce 1999).

Several methods exist to measure innovative performance. There are traditional indicators like patent counting, patent citations, R&D expenditures, scientometric indicators and so on. There are also various typologies developed by Bell and Pavitt (1995), Figueiredo (2001), and Lall (1992). These indicators in an increasing scale identifies different levels of novelty and complexity that firms adopt over time in terms of their processes, products, and services.

R&D performance measurement of firms

There are various measures available measures to map the innovative performance by firms. R&D inputs in terms of manpower, R&D investment are considered as innovation inputs. Patent counts, scholarly literature (journal publications, conference proceedings) new product announcements, and also more specific survey-based measurements are the innovation output measures. Bibliometric indicators are used to map research output in terms of counting the number of published scientific research papers. Patents are generally regarded as the acceptable indicator of innovative output. Beside this, the new product announcement could indicate the level of product innovation. Many studies use a single indicator; for example, R&D expenditure, number of patents, patent citations, or new product announcements. Also, many studies use combination of more than one indicator. However, the diversified use of indicators shows that there are lacks of uniformity and any clear understanding of the concept and measurement of innovative performance (Hagedoorn & Cloodt 2003).

This chapter uses publication and patent counts to measure the innovation potential of firms form these two countries. The publication data is collected from the Scopus database of Elsevier and patent data was collected from Patentscope database of World Intellectual Property Organization (WIPO). Both these data are quite reliable and Patentscope available on the public domain for free of cost.

The firms are selected from the Forbes list of 'GLOBAL 2000' firms. The list is available at (https://www.forbes.com/lists/global2000/#7e84eb915ac0). A total of 10 firms from ICT and 10 firms from pharmaceutical sectors are selected to map the innovation potential of firms with R&D units in India and China. The ICT sector firms are further categorized into three categories. These firms in each category are as follows: Communications Equipment (Cisco Systems, Inc., Hewlett Packard Enterprise Company, Nokia Corporation, Telefonaktiebolaget LM Ericsson), Software & Services industry (International Business Machines Corporation, Microsoft Corporation, Semiconductor equipment industry (Intel Corporation, Qualcomm Technologies, Inc., Samsung Electronics Co Ltd, Texas Instruments Incorporated). There are altogether 10 firms from Pharmaceutical Sector. These firms are; AstraZeneca AB, Bristol Myers Squibb, Eli Lilly & Co., GlaxoSmithKline plc, Johnson & Johnson, Merck & Co., Inc., Novartis AG, Novo Nordisk A/S, Pfizer Inc., Sanofi S.A. The further analysis is based on these 20 firms (10 firms in ICT sector and 10 firms from pharmaceutical sector)

Publication activities of firms

Research published in scholarly journals are considered as important indicator of research output. To map the publication activities of firms', scholarly publication data from the Scopus database of Elsevier science are downloaded. Scopus is an indexing and abstracting database launched in November 2004. According to (Scopus content coverage guide, updated in January 2020), the database covers more than 25,100 journal titles from more than 5,000 international publishers. The database covers global research output in almost all fields of knowledge. It covers scholarly articles in all branches of science, social science, and arts & humanities.

Scopus data can be searched and retrieved based on the affiliation data (using the 70,000 affiliation profiles). According to the Scopus content coverage guide, the 'Scopus Affiliation Identifier' automatically identifies and matches an organization with all of its research output. This tool is particularly relevant for this research because it grouped all firms and their subsidiaries into a single entity. The affiliation search uses the combination of various algorithms and automatically identify and match most relevant records. The records from the selected firms are downloaded from the Affiliation search page of Scopus search interface by entering the respective firms' name.

The document search page opens the search results showing the affiliation names including the firms name and their subsidiaries. The detail search string is given in Appendix I, Appendix II, and Appendix IIII. In the ICT sector, 10 firms are chosen for the study. Table 5.1 shows the scholarly research output of firms from the Scopus database for year 1975-2020.

Table 6. Scholarly research output of firms in ICT and Pharmaceutical sector

Forbes Global Rank	Sl. No	Name of the firm	Total Publications during 1975-2020	Publication from India during 1975-2020	Percentage of total publication from India	Publications from China during 1975-2020	Percentage of total publication from China
		Communications Equipment					
75	1	Cisco Systems, Inc.	4099	195	4.76	228	5.56
709	2	Hewlett Packard Enterprise company	22374	388	1.73	495	2.21
712	3	Nokia Corporation	96652	756	1.83	2253	2.44
293	4	Telefonaktiebolaget LM Ericsson	9870	163	0.78	291	2.33
		Software & Services industry					
59	5	International Business Machines Corporation	114980	3922	3.41	3410	2.97
15	6	Microsoft Corporation	33695	1652	4.90	7298	21.66
		Semiconductor equipment industry					
36	7	Intel Corporation	27913	818	2.93	1576	5.65
206	8	Qualcomm Technologies,	9858	203	2.06	323	3.28

		Inc.					
11	9	Samsung Electronics Co Ltd	17993	176	0.98	322	1.79
341	10	Texas Instruments Incorporated	14392	733	5.09	171	1.19
Pharmaceutical Sector							
161	1	AstraZeneca AB	28610	360	1.26	728	2.54
410	2	Bristol Myers Squibb	19875	301	1.51	295	1.48
186	3	Eli Lilly & Co.	26742	231	0.86	420	1.57
97	4	GlaxoSmithKline plc	50832	557	1.10	645	1.27
34	5	Johnson & Johnson	14926	157	1.05	315	2.11
84	6	Merck & Co., Inc.	43082	183	0.42	596	1.38
65	7	Novartis AG	25287	409	1.62	478	1.89
260	8	Novo Nordisk A/S	8371	104	1.24	215	2.57
58	9	Pfizer Inc.	71528	312	0.44	763	1.07
72	10	Sanofi S.A.	26717	174	0.65	170	0.64

As seen from the table 5.1, in communication equipment industry Cisco Corporation has 228 publications from China. It constitutes about 5.65 per cent of its total publications. Cisco has also about 195 publications from India which is about 4.76 percent of its global publication.

In IT and software service industry Microsoft is the major actor. It has published about 7, 298 research articles which is about 21.66 percent of its global publication.

In semiconductor and Semiconductor Equipment industry, Intel has about 1,576 (about 5.65 percent of its global publications. Texas Instruments has the 733 publications (about 5.09) of its total publication.

From the above table 5.1 and the discussion, it can be observed that firm's publication from both India and China is not significant in comparison to their global publication portfolio. Different firms have different strategy India and China. For example, Microsoft, Intel is active in China whereas Texas Instruments, Cisco are active in India. Firms are using their strength differently to enhance their global strength.

Growth of publications

The growth of publication of firms in ICT sector observe an exponential growth from the year 2000 to 2012. After that, there was a gradual decline in publications in recent years. However, the growth trends shows a positive coorelation in both the cases.

Figure 4. Growth of literatue in ICT and Pharmaceuticle firms from India and China

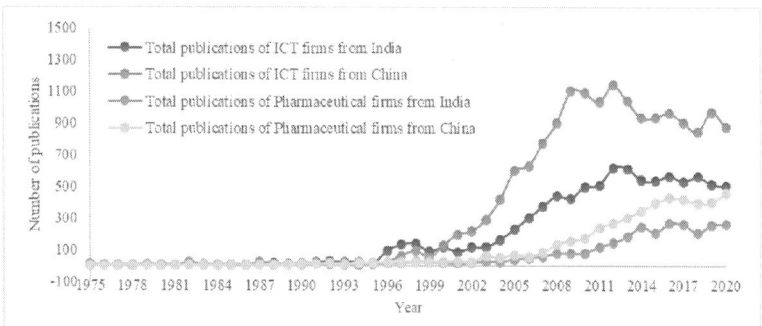

Scholarly research output of firms from pharmaceutical sectors are shown in table 5.1. AstraZeneca has published about 728 (2.54 of their global publication). Johnson & Johnson publish 315 articles (2.11 of global publication) Novo Nordisk A/S publish 215 articles which is about 2.57 of the firm's global publication during that period. From India AstraZeneca AB has 360 articles (1.26 percent), Bristol Myers Squibb has 301(1.51 percent) GlaxoSmithKline plc has 557 articles (1.1 percent), Johnson & Johnson has 157 articles (1.05 percent) Novartis AG has 409 (1.62 percent) and Novo Nordisk A/S has 104 articles

(1.24 percent) of their global publication portfolio. Rest other firms have less than 1 percent publications produced from India. A comparative analysis of publication growth of firms from these two countries shows that over all there is an increase of publications from both India and China, since the early 2000s (Figure 5.1). There was drop of publication in from both the countries in the year 2018. However, there is again a growth of publications since the last two years. From the last couples of years trends, it can be observed that cumulatively about 450 articles are published from China and 250 articles are published from India.

Patenting activities of firms

Patent statistics are considered as an important innovation counts among innovation policy researcher, government decision makers and other interested stakeholders. It is also a matter of interest among economists and policy researchers for a long time (Griliches, 1990). Patent information is increasingly used to analyze the innovation process (Nagaoka et.al., 2010). Advances in ICT and available of patent statistics from the respective countries' patent office globally, have given a new dimension in patent analysis as a proxy measures of innovative activities. Patent bibliometrics are widely used in mapping international patterns of innovative activities amongst firms and their effects on firm performance and industrial dynamics (Pavitt 1985).

However, patent as an innovation indicator is contested by various scholars. It has a number of shortcomings and obvious biasness (Hagedoorn & Cloodt 2003). Among many, the major shortcomings are; *Firstly*, there are differences in patenting behaviors among sectors, for example some sectors observe more patenting activity than other. *Secondly*, there are differences between the large and small firms. Large firms because of their size, file and get approval of more patents than the small firms. *Thirdly*, all patents get the same weight and counted as equivalent. With all these issues, in most of the innovation literature, patent counts are generally accepted as one of the most appropriate indicators for comparing innovative performance of companies in terms of new technologies, new processes and new products. (Hagedoorn & Cloodt 2003).

This chapter considers World Intellectual Property Organization (WIPO) Patent data downloaded from (https://www.wipo.int/patentscope/en/). The PATENTSCOPE database provided by WIPO give access to international Patent Cooperation Treaty (PCT) applications in bibliographic as well as full text format filed by participating national and regional patent offices.

The table 5.2 has given the number of patents granted and filed by the selected ICT firms and pharmaceutical firms. The data has been taken form PATENTSCOPE database with Applicant's name as the respective firm's name. The search was restricted until December 2010. The detail search string is presented in Appendix IV. The Indian and Chinese records are further separated and downloaded in excel comma delaminated format for further analysis.

Patent portfolio of firms

The patenting activity of firms from India and China shows almost similar picture (table 5.2). In Communication Equipment, Industry Telefonaktiebolaget LM Ericsson has 6,992 patents (4, 68 percent) from India. Nokia Corporation has 7,788 patents (8, 01 percent) from China. In Software and service industry, Microsoft is significantly doing patenting both from their Indian and Chinese R&D units. Microsoft Corporation has 4,987 patents (4, 28 percent) from India and 8,997 patents (7, 73 percent) from China.

Table 7. Shows the patent portfolio of firms from India and China.

Forbes Global Rank	Sl. No	Name of the firm	Global Patents filed during 1975-	Patents filed from India during	Percent patent filed from India	Patents filed from China during	Percent patent filed from China

			2020	1975-2020		1975-2020	
		Communications Equipment					
75	1	Cisco Systems, Inc.	27288	484	1.77	1422	5.21
709	2	Hewlett Packard Enterprise company	208011	3413	1.64	5930	2.85
712	3	Nokia Corporation	97220	2887	2.97	7788	8.01
293	4	Telefonaktiebolaget LM Ericsson	149262	6992	4.68	10229	6.85
		Software & Services industry					
59	5	International Business Machines Corporation	211444	812	0.38	3723	1.76
15	6	Microsoft Corporation	116386	4987	4.28	8997	7.73
		Semiconductor equipment industry					
36	7	Intel Corporation	114834	1493	1.30	11372	9.90
341	8	Qualcomm Technologies, Inc.	168165	16780	9.98	14619	8.69
206	9	Samsung Electronics Co Ltd	649747	8583	1.32	57260	8.81
11	10	Texas Instruments Incorporated	47487	43	0.09	1684	3.55
		Pharmaceutical Industry					
161	1	AstraZeneca	31621	1206	3.81	1528	4.83

		AB					
186	3	Bristol Myers Squibb	26050	768	2.95	988	3.79
97	4	Eli Lilly & Co.	39693	398	1.00	758	1.91
34	5	GlaxoSmithKline plc	13977	553	3.96	534	3.82
84	6	Johnson & Johnson	28099	648	2.31	1052	3.74
65	7	Merck & Co., Inc.	36625	406	1.11	689	1.88
260	8	Novartis AG	121550	3205	2.64	4568	3.76
58	9	Novo Nordisk A/S	15895	368	2.32	1047	6.59
72	10	Pfizer Inc.	22003	682	3.10	912	4.14
410	2	Sanofi S.A.	44167	1231	2.79	1522	3.45

From China, all four Semiconductor firms are significant patents in their portfolio. Intel Corporation 11,372 patents (9, 90 percent) Qualcomm Technologies, Inc. 14,619 patents (8, 69 percent) Samsung Electronics Co Ltd 57,260 patents (8, 81 percent) and Texas Instruments Incorporated have about 1,684 patents (3, 55 percent) patents from China.

In semiconductor industry, firms are not that active in terms of patenting from India. It is interesting to note that Texas Instruments Incorporated is the first foreign firms in India but has no patents filed from their India R&D centre.

Figure 5.2 shows the cumulative growth patterns of patents by frims from India and China. There is a significant growth of ICT patents from China from the year 2015 and there an increasing trend of growth. From India in ICT Sector, there was the highest growth of patent in 2016 with a total 8,004 patents. In addition, in the year 2007, there was 4,168 patents from India. However, the nature of growth from India is fluctuating. The reason of drop of patenting from India in recent years is not clear and may require in-depth and further investigation.

Figure 5. Growth of patents of ICT and Pharmaceutical firms from India and China

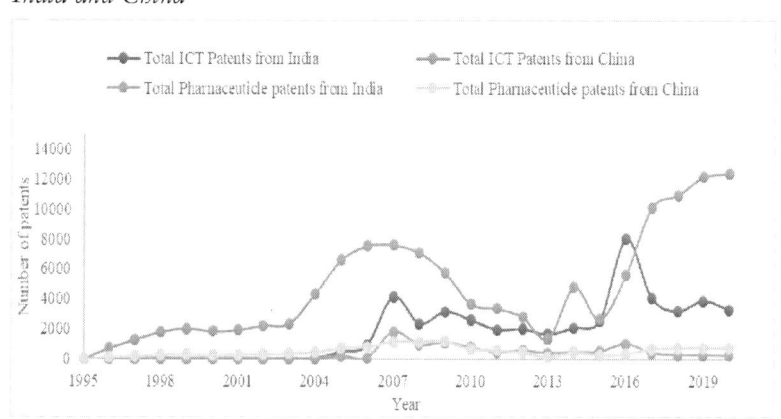

In Pharmaceuticle sector there is no clear trends in patenting both from India and China. The maximum number of patents were filed from India in 2007 with 1,815 patents after that there is decline. Since the last couple of years there is a gradual decline of patents. From China in 2007, there was 1,165 patents, and in 2009, 1,177 patents filed. However, there is growth of patents in recent years.

Innovation from India and China – Selected cases

Beside the evidences from the publication and patent counts, this section will present some evidences of firms' R&D activities in India and China from a few selected cases. These evidences are collected from firm's news published in newspapers, firm's website and other sources. Because of language barrier the Chinese news are collected from the China Daily, the English language newspaper from China.

Johnson & Johnson, the American pharmaceutical MNE introduced the concept of frugal engineering in medical equipment manufacturing in India. It has developed low-cost knee implants and reusable staplers from its India R&D center (Pulakat 2011).

GlaxoSmithKline, the pharmaceutical firm from the UK launched a project named 'Neuro 2020' for neuroscience research in China with various types of partnerships with universities to do neuroscience research and develop products into market for global patients (GSK strengthens China R&D commitment 2016).

The Indian R&D centre of Texas Instruments India, was the first MNE's R&D units started in 1985. The company is doing significant R&D operations from their India centre. It is evident from the recent interview of Biswadip Mitra, the president & managing director of Texas Instruments India that, "Today there's hardly a product at TI worldwide, not touched by innovation done by TI engineers in India. In fact, TI and other chip design houses that followed later, from Intel to Cadence, have collectively made India the chip design hub for the world" (Singh, 2010).

Samsung's R&D centre in Bangalore (SRI-B) is the largest R&D unit outside its home country in Korea. The centre was established in the year in the year 1996. The centre has now become one of the important and advanced R&D centre for Samsung globally. The centre has specialized in artificial intelligence, image processing, multimedia, wireless communications (FE Bureau, 2021). The centre is also specialized in local India-specific innovations particularly in Samsung smartphones for the Indian market. The company develops products based on the growing needs of Indian consumers. A recent innovation the centre has developed is, an 'On Device Search Engine' that helps people to find their pictures and other content on the smartphones easily using natural language search (BW Online Bureau, 2021).

Intel Corporation is also doing R&D from for the global market from their India centre located in Hyderabad. According to a report published in Gadget 360 (an NDTV venture) Nivruti Rai, Country Head of Intel India and VP of Data Center Group, Intel Corporation told,

Over the last 20 years, Intel India has invested significantly in R&D in the country and has been consistently leading in developing the tech ecosystem. We have made significant impact in areas such as Cloud, client, graphics, AI, 5G, and autonomous systems and our new design facility in Hyderabad will enable us to further boost innovation for India and the world" (Indo-Asian News Service, 2019).

In China, Eli Lilly and Innovent, a Chinese domestic pharmaceutical company, jointly launched PD-1 inhibitor (a group of inhibitors for anticancer drugs) to be used for the indication of a main type of non-small cell lung cancer. This jointly developed drug is in the process of getting regulatory approval form the various regulatory bodies overseas. Julio Gay-Ger, president and general manager of Lilly's China, in an interview to China Daily, told that

> We're proud of the drug, which is an episode of 'from China and for the world'. It showed that the value of innovation coming from local Chinese innovation benefits more than Chinese patients. The results should be available worldwide. So definitely this partnership with this new drug, and hopefully with other drugs in the pipeline, we believe we serve patients coming from China to patients worldwide" (Zhou 2021).

Novartis has partnered with local Chinese biotechnology companies for their drug development from their Chinese R&D unit. The products developed in China are now distributed globally. Novartis claimed that products developed in China have benefited patients overseas. Vasant Narasimhan, CEO of Swiss pharmaceutical giant Novartis, during an interview with China Daily told that

> We're really proud to partner with China-based biotech company BeiGene to bring a China-developed PD-1 inhibitor, a cancer treatment, to the rest of the world…. We believe this is an example of how we can be a partner to Chinese companies to bring the innovations from China to patients around the world. The partnership also enables the

101

two sides to combine the PD-1 with a range of Novartis oncology products (Zhou 2021).

Cisco China Research and Development Center (CRDC) was established in the year 2005 is the third largest R&D center of Cisco around the world. The centre has about 2,200 engineers located in Shanghai, Hefei, Shenzhen, Suzhou and Hangzhou. The centre develops various networking technologies both in China and globally. According to Owen Chan, chairman and CEO of Cisco Greater China,

> As Cisco's engine for innovation, CRDC has fully demonstrated our long-term commitment to China through our five-year presence in the country. In line with Cisco's global R&D strategy, CRDC now represents a global research center of excellence, providing innovative technologies, products and solutions for the global market (Cisco's China R&D center celebrates 5th anniversary, 2010).

Ericsson has made its presence in China mainly in manufacturing. The firm's annual R&D investment in China is more than $310 million. It has more than 5,000 employees in various business operation along various cities in China including Beijing, Shanghai, Guangzhou, Nanjing, Chengdu and Shenzhen. Now it is the largest global R&D centre outside its home country Sweden. The China R&D centre is working on 4G, both for TD-LTE and FDD LTE supporting the operators and deployment of 4G LTE networks in China and globally. Moreover, the centre is also working on the global standardization of 5G mobile communications evolution globally from its China R&D centre (Liu, 2015).

Summary

This chapter maps foreign R&D centres in India and China according to their publication and patenting activities. The chapter has also presented selected cases from both the ICT and Pharmaceutical firms' innovation in various technology areas. The patenting and publication pattern shows that there is a growth of patenting from their foreign R&D centres. The growth is significantly co-related with the global growth of the firm's patenting. However, the number of publications is significantly lower in terms of global patenting by the firms. Patenting activity of foreign firms shows that the global patenting and patenting from China is not co-related. It means that the patenting from China is not increasing with that of the global growth.

The firms are also doing latest cutting-edge technology from their overseas R&D base. However, it is still not clear in terms of both the global technology development as well as socially applicable technology and its relevance. The further in-depth investigation may lead to a clear and better picture.

CHAPTER VI. LINKAGES AND KNOWLEDGE SPILLOVER

Introduction

In the present-day globalization, the acquisition of new organizational knowledge *across borders* (Kogut & Zander 2003) is becoming important for MNEs. New knowledge across border gives multinational firms the basis for organizational renewal and sustainable competitive advantage (Nakamura 2003). However, it is a matter of concern for the interested stakeholders on the effects of multinational enterprises (MNEs) form both the home as well as host economies' perspectives (Giroud & Scott-Kennel 2006).

Earlier chapters dealt with the fact that MNEs are the major actors in knowledge transfer in developing host countries (Saliola & Zanfei 2009). Innovation and international business literature observed that FDI is one of the ways to international knowledge spillovers. Subsidiaries of foreign MNEs are the medium through which technological knowledge flows across borders. However, empirical evidence of the MNEs and their knowledge transfer mechanisms and its effectiveness, in comparison to other economic institutions is limited (Almeida et al., 2002). For foreign subsidiaries to be channels of international spillovers, these subsidiaries need to source their expertise internationally and transfer the technology to the local economy (Veugelers & Cassiman 2004). Because of their big size and resources, firms possess superior knowledge and it can cross geographical boundaries by transferring knowledge between countries (Almeida 2002 et al.).

However, another new dimension, i.e., the geographical "stickiness" of knowledge is getting recent attention among the innovation studies researchers. A stream of literature in the field of international management have emphasized on the various options and benefits of cross-border innovation projects within the MNEs R&D network (Zander & Sölvell 2000; Saliola & Zanfei 2009).

MNEs firms go abroad to acquire technological knowledge from different knowledge hubs spread across the globe. Knowledge has unique characteristics because of its tacit component. It is sticky and located within narrow spatial boundaries. Various regional clusters, like Silicon Valley in the US (Teece, 1992), Bangalore software cluster in India (Walcott & Heitzman, 2006), Zuncunguansun software cluster in China (Zhou & Xin, 2003) are attracting new investment from domestic as well as foreign multinationals to locate their business in these clusters to source knowledge from these knowledge clusters (Almeida, 1996). From the host countries' policy perspectives, it is host countries look for most investment in FDI also interested achieving sustainable economic development by means of increasing FDI. One of the means of getting benefits from FDI is through production linkages between foreign affiliates and domestic firms (UNCTAD 2001).

There is a strong opinion among scholars, policy and decision makers that FDI is the possible mechanism for development in developing countries. Among the many ways of benefits, the most prominent mechanism is the "linkages" between foreign firms and domestic firms in host countries. MNEs linkage in various forms with the local actors is crucial for the local economic development. Linkages with foreign subsidiaries generate positive externalities and knowledge spillovers (Blomstro¨m & Kokko 1998, UNCTAD 2001). Therefore, governments in both developed and developing countries promotes FDI. Many host countries have reduced barriers to FDI by implementing favorable policies for the firms to operate in the host county. In addition, many of them have offered special incentives to attract foreign firms and foster relationships between multinationals and local firms. Surprisingly, however, the empirical literature has not been able to confirm the existence of positive externalities from FDI to host countries (Alfaro et. al. 2004).

MNEs linkages in a host country can be of three types. The linkages can be *backward, forward or horizontal*. The *backward linkages* are the process where foreign affiliates acquire goods or services from the domestic firm. *Forward linkages* are the relationship where foreign affiliates sell goods or services to domestic firms. *Horizontal linkages* involve interactions with domestic firms engaged in various competing activities. Research shows that various types of linkages among the foreign firms with that of local entities of a host country have the major impact on the capability and resource development of these firms. Hence, domestic firm's capability building depends upon the scope, quantity and quality of linkages formed with foreign-local interaction (Giroud & Scott-Kennel, 2009).

In the global arena, the complexities increase in scope as MNEs contend with the cross-border knowledge transfers and the challenge of renewing organizational skills in various diverse settings (Inkpen 1998). There may be many different types of 'Strategic alliances', such as joint ventures (JVs), licensing agreements, distribution and supply agreements, R&D partnerships, and technical exchanges. A clear understanding of the relationship between MNEs strategies and local linkage is essential for the developing countries to formulate suitable policies to reap maximum benefits from FDI by MNEs (UNCTAD, 2001; Hansen et al 2009).

Multinational Firms' Embeddedness with the local Innovation System

MNE's subsidiaries are embedded themselves within different actors and knowledge networks in the host country. Firms develop linkages to accumulate their capabilities for innovation in products, processes, and services. These types of linkages strengthen a firm's competitive advantage in the global market (Figueiredo 2011).

MNE subsidiaries embedded in a network of specific business relationships (Andersson & Forsgren 1996). Embeddedness is the structure of a network in social context and the partners' relations affecting economic actions. Its outcomes as well as the behaviors in the network based on various types of partnership (Gulati 1998, 1999; Duysters & Lemmens 2003). Firms usually do local search for forming their alliances. The partner selection process is time-consuming and cost involved. Network formation advances with the formation of new technology relationships, building on the experience with existing ties. Through preferential collaboration, firms embedded in densely connected networks of relations.

Additionally, firms very occasionally work in isolation to build their assets, but works in an interactive way with other actors of the innovation system (Gulati, 1998). However, there are variations in the pattern of interaction of the firms with the different actors in the innovation ecosystem. This variation is due to the firm's embeddedness with different actors in their setting to create knowledge for competitive performance (Figueiredo 2011, Ariffin (2000). This chapter will examine the firms' embeddedness with different actors in the innovation system from co-authorship of the scholarly publication. Joint patents are also used to examine the collaboration among various entities. This chapter examines the linkages using various indicators (actor level) from Social Network Analysis tools.

Social Network Analysis

Social Network Analysis (SNA) is a method to represent the relationships among different actors in a system. SNA is represented as points (or vertices or actors) and lines (or edges or relationships) and the associations among them. The points denote entities, organizations, or positions, while the lines denote the relations that connect those (Scott & Stokman, 2015). Using SNA tools, various type of relationship can be represented. The relationships may be the communication among various actors, friendship and so on. The lines show the relationship can include various attributes and can be directed (e.g., passing information) or undirected (e.g., joint collaboration) (Steketee, Miyaoka, & Spiegelman 2015).

SNA broadly use two level of measurement to understand the role of various actor in a network. These measures are Node-level Statistical Measures and Network-level Statistical Measures (Tabassum, Pereira, and Fernandes & Gama 2018). These measurements are used to understand the role of nodes in the network. The node level analysis explores various centrality measures to understand the position of a node within the overall structure of the graph. The latter macro level or network level measures allows the assess overall structure of the network (Newman 2018).

In a Social Network, various Centrality measures are the used to quantify the importance of a node in a network. For this study three actor's node level centrality measures Degree, Closeness Betweenness are considered.

Degree is the number of edges connected to a node. The number of edges or connections shows the importance of a node in the network. The greater number of connections a node has the more powerful is the node in the network. Closeness measures shows how well a node is connected to every other node in the network. Betweenness shows the importance of a node by placing itself in between other nodes. It is the number of shortest paths from one node to the other. The higher betweenness value of a node in the networks shows the importance of the node in the network because it is important in terms of flow of the information from one node to another node in the network. Eigenvector is a measure of node importance in a network. If a node close to the other node, which has higher value, means that node is also important in that network. These four measures will be used in this chapter to show various actors' importance in the network.

The analytical framework of local embeddedness is examined with various measures of Social Network Analysis (SNA) tools. Both the patent and publication data are used to find the collaboration patterns among firms and the local entities. The Scopus bibliographic data is downloaded in the export refine format. Form that data affiliation information is collected and the network graphs are drawn using the open-source software Gephi and UCINET. These two open-source software is useful to draw network maps among various actors. UCINET has inbuilt software package Net Draw used to do the graph analysis including various centrality measures.

Collaboration of Firms in India and China

The linkages of pharmaceutical firms with the local entities are discussed in this section. This section will draw the evidences of various types of linkages from various press statements, newspaper reports and other sources.

Pharmaceutical firms' linkages in India

In recent years, global pharmaceutical firms with operation in India prefer tie-ups with the Indian firms to acquisitions. In the year 2012, in a press statement Pfizer MD Kewal Handa said, *"The reasons for partnerships are many. But I see two primary reasons. The Indian market is getting more regulated and thus offers more scope for multinationals. Secondly, Big Pharma are finding more value addition by tying up with Indian companies"* (Amirapu, 2012). Indian firms see this phenomenon as an opportunity of collaboration with foreign firms. Global MNEs find it difficult to sustain their growth because of fast exhausting pipeline of drugs, expiry of existing patents and the cost involved in developing new products. There are many examples available from the news reports that can substantiate this claim. For example, Pfizer has formed a number of collaborations with the local university or institutes. However, as it is evident that industry academia linkage is comparatively week. Foreign firms mainly bank on the strength of Indian pharmaceutical firms. Many Indian pharmaceutical firms conduct Phase I or early Phase II of clinical trials and then transfer them to MNEs. There are many examples of these kinds of deals. In the year 2007, Eli Lilly signed agreement with Glenmark for Clinical Trial of osteoarthritis drug, GRC 6211 (BS Reporter, 2013). Eli Lilly had signed deals in 2009 with Piramal Life Sciences Ltd for Phase I trial of a new experimental drug molecule P2202. This drug was experimented for diabetes metabolic syndrome in Canada (BS Reporter 2013). In February 2013, Merck signed discovery and clinical development agreement to develop drug candidates in metabolic diseases with Advinus. It is a Tata Group drug discovery company founded in 2005(Advinus, Merck establish drug discovery collaboration 2013). In 2007, Glaxo SmithKline extended its earlier agreement with Ranbaxy to take candidate molecules through the early stages of development (Ranbaxy, GSK Enter New R&D Pact 2007). Wyeth works in partnership with GVK Biosciences (Businesswire India 2008) and Eli Lilly with Jubilant Organosys (ET Bureau, 2009). Nicholas Piramal India has signed a pact with Merck & Co to discover and develop two new cancer drugs up to the initial stage of clinical trials (PharmaTimes 2007).

It is mentioned in the previous chapter that scholarly publication data was downloaded from the Scopus data of Elsevier science. From the downloaded data, the affiliation information was collected and plotted in matrix form to draw the network map of the firms. The co-authorship collaboration network of firms has two distinct components from India and China respectively. A social network map of the firm's collaboration is presented in Figure 6. 1.

Figure 6. Network map of pharmaceutical firms' co-authorship in India

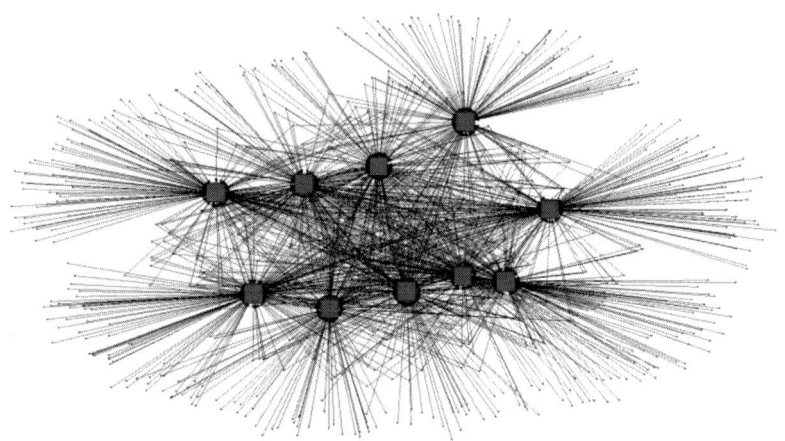

The table 6.1 shows the different centrality measures of pharmaceutical firms' linkages in India. The network map was drawn as two-mode network where the foreign firms are collaborating with other entities. The table 6.1 shows the various centrality measures including the degree, betweenness, closeness and eigenvector centrality measures. In terms of degree centrality measures with decreasing values are as follows; Eli Lilly, AstraZeneca, Pfizer, Sanofi, Bristol Myers Squibb, Novo Nordisk, Johnson & Johnson, Merck & Co., GlaxoSmithKline and Novartis. However, looking at the publication profiles both from India and from China, there is not much difference in the centrality measures and its value. Moreover, only 160-affiliation information have been collected from the Scopus 'export refine' format. Therefore, there is a cut-offs numbers in terms of network structure construction.

There are altogether 2,788 publications of the firms available in the Scopus database during the period 1975-2020. These firms are collaborating with other entities for their coauthored publication. The collaboration map is drawn with the firms and 470 other entities. The firms collaborating with the other entities are in 'rows' of the Matrix. Among the top 10 collaborating entities the following, Harvard Medical School, Merck & Co., Inc., National Institutes of Health NIH, University of California, San Francisco, University of Washington, Amgen Incorporated, AstraZeneca, GlaxoSmithKline, Inserm, Karolinska Institutet and so on. Therefore, it is evident from the table 6.1 that foreign pharmaceutical firms' local collaboration with the entities in Indian innovation system is not prominent.

Table 8. Centrality measures of pharmaceutical firms' co-authorship in India

Sl. No.	ID	*Mode	Degree	Betweenness	Closeness	Eigenvector
1.	Eli Lilly	Columns	155	42938,12	1718	0,051
2.	AstraZeneca	Columns	153	31172,68	1722	0,058
3.	Pfizer	Columns	153	31485,02	1722	0,058
4.	Sanofi	Columns	152	37718,56	1724	0,05
5.	Bristol Myers Squibb	Columns	152	43183,4	1724	0,048
6.	Novo Nordisk	Columns	152	48041,25	1724	0,039
7.	Johnson & Johnson	Columns	150	44803,68	1728	0,045
8.	Merck & Co., Inc.	Columns	150	27726,87	1728	0,059
9.	GlaxoSmithKline	Columns	149	29883,5	1730	0,058
10.	Novartis	Columns	144	36552,01	1740	0,049
11.	Harvard Medical School	Rows	10	3353,474	1348	0,123
12.	Merck & Co., Inc.	Rows	10	3353,474	1348	0,123
13.	National Institutes of Health NIH	Rows	10	3353,474	1348	0,123
14.	University of California, San Francisco	Rows	10	3353,474	1348	0,123
15.	University of Washington	Rows	10	3353,474	1348	0,123
16.	Amgen Incorporated	Rows	9	2712,832	1430	0,112

17.	AstraZeneca	Rows	9	2114,554	1474	0,114
18.	GlaxoSmithKline	Rows	9	2114,554	1474	0,114
19.	Inserm	Rows	9	2601,391	1452	0,111
20.	Karolinska Institutet	Rows	9	2434,433	1462	0,113

Further analysis of the network structure shows that firms are collaborating with their headquarters and other entities globally rather than the local entities for example (universities or research institutes in India. Moreover, it is discussed in the previous chapter that firms' publication profile is not that much either from India or from China. Therefore, it can be concluded that although firms are developing linkages in terms of joint development or joint venture, it is not reflected in joint publication.

Pharmaceutical firms' linkages in China

MNEs are leading an aggressive M&A strategy to capture Chinese market. Many biopharmaceutical companies use mergers and acquisitions (M&A) as a part of its China growth strategy. In this way, firms complete its industry value chain and expand into the grassroots market at comparatively lower cost. In addition to the organic growth most of the firms seeks M&A for the development of the company over the long term. For example, *Novartis AG* acquire 85 percent stake in Zhejiang-based Tianyuan Bio-Pharmaceutical Co Ltd for 850 million yuan (Tang 2011). *Sanofi-Aventis SA* acquired *BMP Sunstone Corporation* for approximately $521 million in the largest M&A deal in China's pharmaceutical industry (Wang 2011).

Similarly, a number of firms have formed alliances with the local firms in China. For example, Pfizer Inc signed a memorandum of understanding (MOU) with Chinese firm Zhejiang Hisun Pharmaceuticals to establish a joint venture. This MoU aimed to strengthen the capability for both the firms to reach more patients with high-quality and low-cost medicines in the branded generics medicine (Pfizer 2011). Pfizer and Jilin Guoyuan Animal Health Company formed a joint venture to strengthen its R&D capabilities in animal health care in China (Pfizer 2011).

Beside the newspaper reports, news announcements and other source, this section tried to get evidences from the co-authored articles published in scholarly journals. Scientific collaboration has increased among nations and research institutions in recent years. Bibliometric analysis of co-authored scientific articles is one of the measures used in mapping the collaborations among different actors (Melin & Persson 1996; Katz & Martin 1997).

Co-authorship collaboration network of the selected firms are drawn using UCINET and NET Draw software (Figure 6.1). In China, the 10 selected pharmaceutical firms collaborated with 568 different types of actors. The whole network has 577 nodes and 1482 ties with them.

Figure 7. Network map of pharmaceutical firms' co-authorship in China

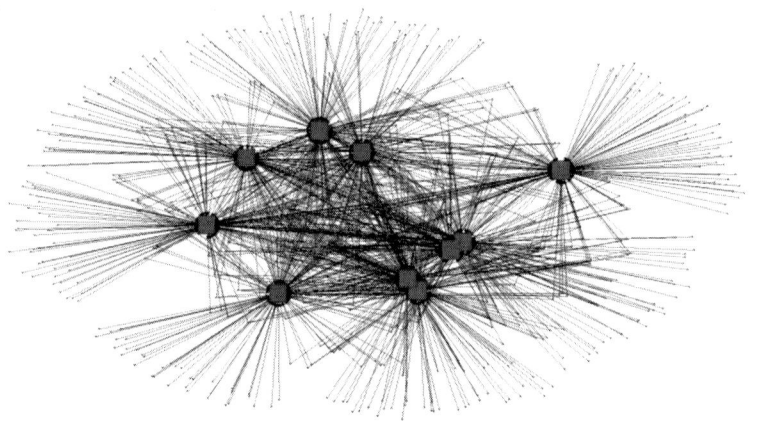

The various actor level centrality measures show in table 6.2. In terms of degree centrality measures the firm's degree of collaboration in decreasing orders are as follows. Novo Nordisk, Bristol Myers Squibb, Eli Lilly, Merck & Co., AstraZeneca, Sanofi, Pfizer, GlaxoSmithKline, Johnson &

Johnson, Novartis. The top 10 collaborating actors in terms of degree centrality are as follows; Peking University, Fudan University, Chinese Academy of Sciences, Chinese University of Hong Kong, Karolinska Institutet, Harvard Medical School, Chinese Academy of Medical Sciences & Peking Union Medical College, Capital Medical University, University of Toronto, Brigham and Women's Hospital. Therefore, it is evident from the network analysis that Chinese institutes also play important roles in joint research and publications with various actors in the innovation system.

Table 9. Centrality measures of pharmaceutical firms' co-authorship in China

Sl. No	ID	*Mode	Degree	Betweenness	Closeness	Eigenvector
1.	Novo Nordisk	Columns	153	37777,398	1413	0,04
2.	Bristol Myers Squibb	Columns	150	29467,867	1419	0,053
3.	Eli Lilly	Columns	150	22491,607	1419	0,058
4.	Merck & Co., Inc.	Columns	150	20276,289	1419	0,064
5.	AstraZeneca	Columns	149	22657,025	1421	0,058
6.	Sanofi	Columns	149	30377,607	1421	0,053
7.	Pfizer	Columns	148	19507,818	1423	0,062
8.	GlaxoSmithKline	Columns	146	19256,254	1427	0,062
9.	Johnson & Johnson	Columns	145	28252,656	1429	0,053
10.	Novartis	Columns	142	26665,561	1435	0,051
11.	Peking University	Rows	10	1765,841	1142	0,116
12.	Fudan University	Rows	10	1765,841	1142	0,116
13.	Chinese Academy of Sciences	Rows	10	1765,841	1142	0,116
14.	Chinese University of Hong Kong	Rows	10	1765,841	1142	0,116
15.	Karolinska Institutet	Rows	10	1765,841	1142	0,116
16.	Harvard Medical School	Rows	10	1765,841	1142	0,116
17.	Chinese Academy of Medical Sciences & Peking Union Medical College	Rows	10	1765,841	1142	0,116
18.	Capital Medical University	Rows	10	1765,841	1142	0,116

| 19. | University of Toronto | Rows | 10 | 1765,841 | 1142 | 0,116 |
| 20. | Brigham and Women's Hospital | Rows | 10 | 1765,841 | 1142 | 0,116 |

ICT Firms' Linkages

MNEs have developed linkages with different actor of innovation system in India and China. This section will describe some of the examples of different types of linkages with different actors of innovation system. Among the communication equipment firms, Motorola has a long association with China. Motorola (China) Electronics Ltd. (MCEL) set up its first R&D center in China in 1993. It is the first multinational R&D center in China. Motorola China Research and Development Institute (MCRDI) has over 1500 R&D staff and 15 R&D centers in different centres in China. Freescale semiconductor a spinoff from Motorola has 4 R&D centers and about 200 employees. Now MCRDI is the biggest multinational R&D institute in China. MCRDI has several joint programs with local universities, companies and government agencies (Motorola opens new R&D centre, 2006).

Microsoft formed an alliance with BesTV New Media Co, a Chinese Internet protocol TV service provider in 2013. With this alliance, Microsoft entered into China's video gaming market (Shen J, 2013). Microsoft formed alliance with Chinese company Amoi Electronics to enter into the communications and consumer electronics markets in China (Liu, 2005). IBM formed alliance with Chinese software firm Kingsoft to develop office software for different operating systems (IBM, Kingsoft form alliance, 2003).

The US chip giant Qualcomm Inc formed an alliance with Chinese firm Huawei Technologies. In this alliance, both the companies formed a global patent license agreement and Qualcomm pay a catch-up payment of $1.8 billion to Huawei (Ma 2020).

Collaboration of ICT firm's joint publication with various actors in India

The joint publication-based evidence from the scholarly literature is collected from the Scopus database of the selected ICT firms. The affiliation information of firms is collected from the downloaded records. The affiliation information is then plotted in Matrix form to draw the network map of the firm's co-authorship collaboration map. Figure 6.3 shows the collaboration among the different actors. The whole network has 819 nodes and 1483 ties among them.

Figure 8. Network map of ICT firms' co-authorship in India

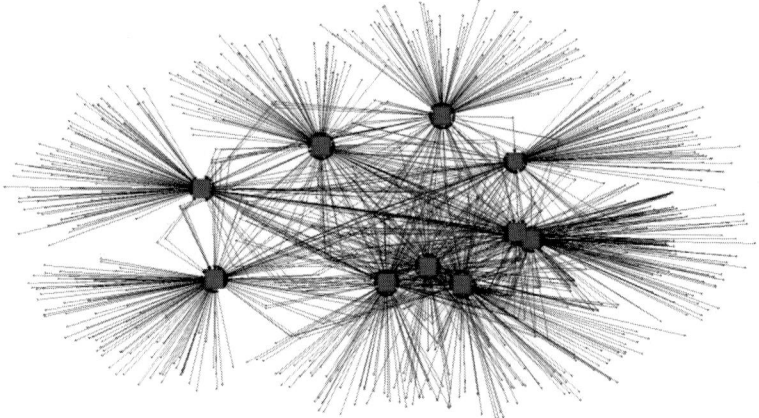

The table 6.3 shows different centrality measures of firms. The degree centrality measures of firms in terms of decreasing value of centrality measures are as follows; Texas Instruments, Ericsson, Microsoft, Nokia, Qualcomm, Cisco, Intel, Hewlett Packard, IBM, Samsung. It can be observed from the table below that in terms of degree centrality measures there is not much variations of the firms' collaboration networks in India.

Among the collaborating entities the degree centrality measures in terms of decreasing values are as follows; Birla Institute of Technology and Science, Pilani, Indian Institute of Science, Indian Institute of Technology Delhi, Indian Institute of Technology Madras, Indian Institute of Technology, Bombay, Intel Corporation, IBM India Pvt Ltd, IEEE, Indian Institute of Technology Kanpur, and Indian Institute of Technology Kharagpur. Therefore, it is evident form the ICT firms' linkages in India, few premier educational institutes are prominent in collaboration.

Table 10. Centrality measures of ICT firms' co-authorship in India

Sl. No	ID	*Mode	Degree	Betweenness	Closeness	Eigenvector
1.	Texas Instruments	Columns	155	65532,97	2135	0,046
2.	Ericsson	Columns	154	79983,06	2137	0,026
3.	Microsoft	Columns	152	53266,5	2141	0,055
4.	Nokia	Columns	151	50545,88	2143	0,057
5.	Qualcomm	Columns	151	75729,23	2143	0,036
6.	CISCO	Columns	150	75823,78	2145	0,032
7.	Intel	Columns	150	39476,37	2145	0,06
8.	Hewlett Packard	Columns	147	39264,04	2151	0,058
9.	IBM	Columns	146	40018,93	2153	0,061
10.	Samsung	Columns	127	54320,12	2191	0,036
11.	Birla Institute of Technology and Science, Pilani	Rows	10	8325,297	1626	0,131
12.	Indian Institute of Science	Rows	10	8325,297	1626	0,131
13.	Indian Institute of Technology Delhi	Rows	10	8325,297	1626	0,131
14.	Indian Institute of Technology Madras	Rows	10	8325,297	1626	0,131
15.	Indian Institute of Technology, Bombay	Rows	10	8325,297	1626	0,131
16.	Intel Corporation	Rows	10	8325,297	1626	0,131
17.	IBM India Pvt Ltd	Rows	9	5950,866	1808	0,121
18.	IEEE	Rows	9	5134,037	1816	0,124
19.	Indian Institute	Rows	9	5134,037	1816	0,124

	of Technology Kanpur					
20.	Indian Institute of Technology Kharagpur	Rows	9	5134,037	1816	0,124

The co-authorship collaboration network of the selected firms in China has 746 nodes and 1512 ties. The network map of co-authorship collaboration map is shown in figure 6. 4. In terms of degree centrality measures the firm's degree in decreasing order are as follows; Texas Instruments, Qualcomm, Cisco, Nokia, Microsoft, Hewlett Packard, Ericsson, Intel, Samsung, IBM.

Figure 9. Network map of ICT firms' co-authorship in China

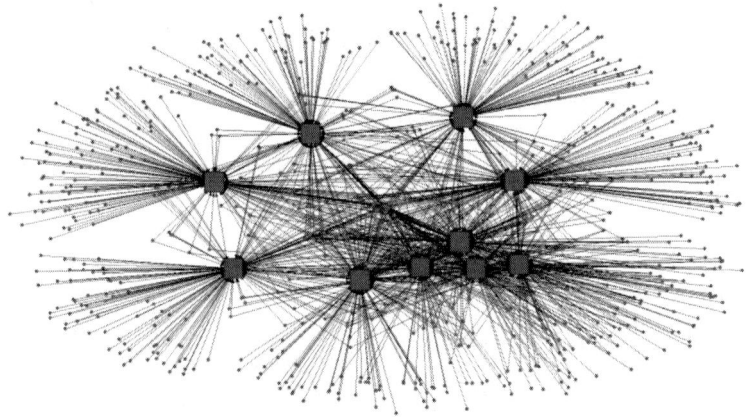

The actor level centrality measures are presented in Table 6.4. The actor level centrality measures of the collaborating entities are in decreasing orders are as follows; Chinese Academy of Sciences, Fudan University, Huazhong University of Science and Technology, Intel Corporation, Ministry of Education China, Peking University, Shanghai Jiao Tong University, Tsinghua University, University of Electronic Science and Technology of China, University of Science and Technology of China, Zhejiang University, Beijing Institute of Technology, Beijing University of Posts and

Telecommunications and so on. It is evident from the table 6.4 that a number of firms in China are actively collaborating with Chinese universities and research institutes for doing joint R&D in China.

Table 11. Centrality measures of ICT firms' co-authorship in China

Sl. No	ID	*Mode	Degree	Betweenness	Closeness	Eigenvector
1.	Texas Instruments	Columns	156	64245,13	1914	0,04
2.	Qualcomm	Columns	155	52786,82	1916	0,049
3.	CISCO	Columns	154	63068,97	1918	0,038
4.	Nokia	Columns	154	43546,58	1918	0,057
5.	Microsoft	Columns	153	31406,16	1920	0,063
6.	Hewlett Packard	Columns	152	36869,85	1922	0,053
7.	Ericsson	Columns	151	59303,19	1924	0,038
8.	Intel	Columns	148	29701,64	1930	0,06
9.	Samsung	Columns	145	53262,85	1936	0,041
10.	IBM	Columns	144	29292,77	1938	0,061
11.	Chinese Academy of Sciences	Rows	10	4818,07	1480	0,124
12.	Fudan University	Rows	10	4818,07	1480	0,124
13.	Huazhong University of Science and Technology	Rows	10	4818,07	1480	0,124
14.	Intel Corporation	Rows	10	4818,07	1480	0,124
15.	Massachusetts Institute of Technology	Rows	10	4818,07	1480	0,124
16.	Ministry of Education China	Rows	10	4818,07	1480	0,124
17.	Peking University	Rows	10	4818,07	1480	0,124
18.	Shanghai Jiao Tong University	Rows	10	4818,07	1480	0,124
19.	Tsinghua University	Rows	10	4818,07	1480	0,124
20.	University of Electronic Science and Technology of China	Rows	10	4818,07	1480	0,124
21.	University of Science and Technology of China	Rows	10	4818,07	1480	0,124

22.	Zhejiang University	Rows	10	4818,07	1480	0,124
23.	Beijing Institute of Technology	Rows	9	3244,58	1640	0,115
24.	Beijing University of Posts and Telecommunications	Rows	9	4034,99	1526	0,111
25.	Georgia Institute of Technology	Rows	9	3244,58	1640	0,115
26.	IEEE	Rows	9	3603,48	1604	0,114
27.	Nanyang Technological University	Rows	9	3341,38	1642	0,114
28.	Nokia Corporation	Rows	9	4034,99	1526	0,111
29.	University of Southern California	Rows	9	3244,58	1640	0,115

Collaboration in Patents

Collaboration in research has various manifestation. Among the various output measures of R&D, joint patents are one of the empirical evidences to support the collaboration and linkages of firms with various actors in the innovation system (Kim & Song, 2007). Recent studies of alliances, particularly the technology-based alliances, have investigated the association between alliances and innovation by looking at patents of individual firms as a reliable indicator of innovation output (Hagedoorn, 2003; Hagedoorn, Kranenburg & Osborn, 2003). This chapter is looking at the joint patents of selected ICT and Pharmaceutical firms by looking at the joint patents resulting from the alliances.

It was mentioned in the previous chapters that patent data was downloaded from the Patentscope database of World Intellectual Property Organization WIPO. WIPO is the global forum of 193 member states looking after the intellectual property (IP) services, policy, information and cooperation. The organization's mandate, governing structure are set out in the WIPO Convention in 1967 (https://www.wipo.int/about-wipo/en/).

Patent data was searched from the Patentscope website using the respective firm's name in the Applicant's name in the search filed (patentscope.wipo.int/search/en/structuredSearch.jsf) For example search string for the patent records of AstraZeneca was searcher using the following search string PA:(AstraZeneca) AND DP: [01.01.1975 TO 31.12.2020]. The retrieved records again filtered using the respective countries name. For example, the firm's Indian patent data was separated. The records downloaded from the website using the comma-delimited format for further analysis. From the downloaded records "Applicants", names separated for collaboration analysis for joint patents.

It is already discussed in the previous chapter that the firms' patents are very less compared to their global portfolio. From the selected firms patent portfolio in pharmaceutical sector GlaxoSmithKline has about 553 patents (3.96 percent) AstraZeneca AB 1,206 patents (3.82 percent) and Pfizer Inc. 628 patents (3.1 percent) from India. The collaborative patents show that from GlaxoSmithKline, among 553 patents only 58 patents are collaborative patents. Merck & Co., Inc. has 406 patents from India and among these total patents, 58 patents are collaborative patents. Hence, it is evident from the table 6.5 that selected firm's collaboration with the other entities are not that much.

Table 12. Joint patents of firms from India and China

Forbes Global Rank in 2021	Sl. No	Name of the firm	Global Patents 1975-2020	Patents from India	Percentage of patents from India	Collaborative patents	Percentage	Patents from China	Percentage of patents from China	Collaborative patents	percentage of collaborative patent
		Communications Equipment									
75	1	Cisco Systems, Inc.	27288	484	1,77	3	0,62	1422	5,21	1295	91
709	2	Hewlett Packard Enterprise company	208011	3413	1,64	96	2,81	5930	2,85	4797	81
712	3	Nokia Corporation	97220	2887	2,97	58	2,01	7788	8,01	6957	89
293	4	Telefonaktiebolaget LM Ericsson	149262	6992	4,68	34	0,49	10229	6,85	9429	92
		Software & Services									

		industry								
59	5	International Business Machines Corporation	211444	812	0,38	37	4,56	3723	1,76	2769	74
15	6	Microsoft Corporation	116386	4987	4,28	1	0,02	8997	7,73	7496	83
		Semiconductor equipment industry									
36	7	Intel Corporation	114834	1493	1,30	5	0,33	11372	9,90	9734	86
206	10	Qualcomm Technologies, Inc.	168165	16780	9,98	15	0,09	14619	8,69	12066	83
11	8	Samsung Electronics Co Ltd	649747	8583	1,32	109	1,27	57260	8,81	51098	89
341	9	Texas Instruments Incorporated	47487	43	0,09	0	0,00	1684	3,55	1400	83
		Pharmaceuticals									
161	1	AstraZeneca AB	31621	1206	3,81	99	8,21	1528	4,83	1472	96
410	3	Bristol Myers Squibb	26050	768	2,95	48	6,25	988	3,79	885	90
186	4	Eli Lilly & Co.	39693	398	1,00	14	3,52	758	1,91	700	92
97	5	GlaxoSmithKline plc	13977	553	3,96	58	10,49	534	3,82	376	70
34	6	Johnson & Johnson	28099	648	2,31	10	1,54	1052	3,74	923	88
84	7	Merck & Co., Inc.	36625	406	1,11	58	14,29	689	1,88	674	98
65	8	Novartis AG	121550	3205	2,64	273	8,52	4568	3,76	3867	85
260	9	Novo Nordisk A/S	15895	368	2,32	11	2,99	1047	6,59	902	86
58	10	Pfizer Inc.	22003	682	3,10	42	6,16	912	4,14	874	96
72	2	Sanofi S.A.	44167	1231	2,79	88	7,15	1522	3,45	1180	78

Patent collaboration networks in pharmaceutical industry

A Network Analysis was conducted using the social network analysis tools to understand the dynamics of various actors and their collaboration patterns in the collaboration.

Pharmaceutical firms' joint patent from India

Among the total 9,465 patents of 10 pharmaceutical firms in this sample, 701 patents (about 7 percent) are joint patents. Merck & Co., Inc. has 406 patents and among this total number of patent 58 patents (14.29 patents) and joint patents. GlaxoSmithKline plc has 553 patents and 58(10, 49 percent) are joint patents. Table 6.5 shows the total patents and the joint patents from India and China respectively. Table 6.6 and figure 6.5 shows the network graph and the actor level network statistics. The network has 371 nodes and 384 ties among them. The largest component is formed by 7 firms and Merck & Co formed a different component.

Figure 10. Network map of pharmaceutical firms' patent network in India

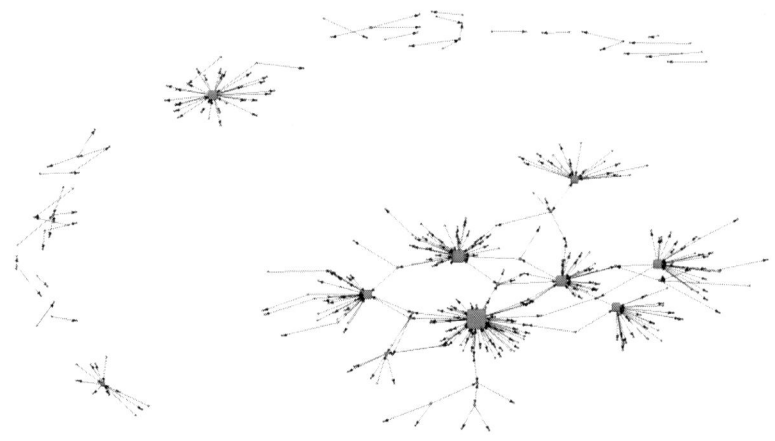

Table 6.6 shows that actor level network statistics. Novartis has the highest degree followed by GlaxoSmithKline, AstraZeneca, Merck, Sanofi, Wyeth (acquired by Pfizer), Bristol Myers Squibb, Syngenta, Eli Lilly and Novo Nordisk. Indian research institutes, universities and other entities are not that active in collaboration. Only Council of Scientific and Industrial research have limited collaboration with other.

Table 13. Centrality measure of pharmaceutical firms' collaborative patents in India

Sl. No.	ID	Degree	Betweenness	Closeness	Eigenvector
1	Novartis	65	19170,69	40115	0,39
2	GlaxoSmithKline	38	10718,94	40177	0,02
3	AstraZeneca	32	15611,98	40141	0,054
4	Merck & co Inc.	29	463,00	125802	0
5	Sanofi	28	7495,15	40369	0,022
6	Wyeth	27	6702	40437	0,004
7	Bristol Myers Squibb	26	6159,85	40352	0,026
8	Syngenta Participations Ag	22	5313	40650	0
9	Eli Lilly and company	11	55	133200	0
10	Novo Nordisk a/s	8	1328,50	40549	0,021

Pharmaceutical firms' joint patent from China

China's pharmaceutical industry is one of the largest emerging industries in the country (Ren & Su, 2015). Therefore, number of patents are comparatively more than India. Table 6.5 shows the number of patents, joint patents and so on. Among the total 13,598 patents retrieved from the sample firms of this study, 11, 853 patents (about 87 percent) are joint patents. AstraZeneca has 1528 patents and among the total patent 1472 (96 percent) are joint patents. Pfizer Inc. has 912 patents 874 (96 percent) are joint patents. However, the detail analysis of the joint patents show that firms are collaborating with their subsidiary located in China.

Figure 11. Network map of pharmaceutical firms' patent network in China

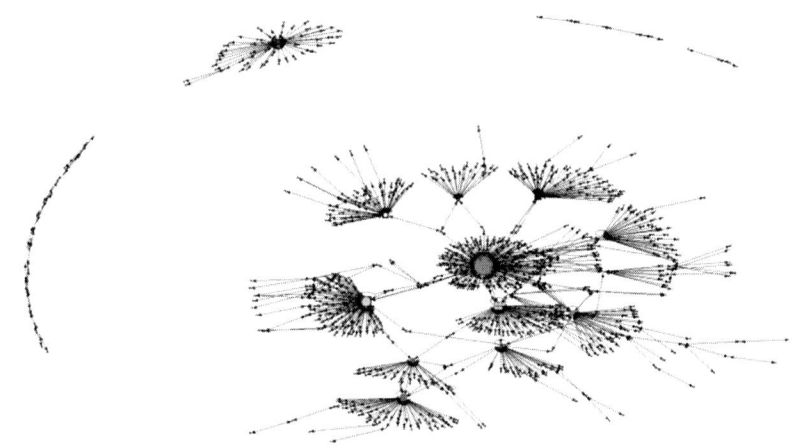

The patent collaboration map drawn using Social Network Analysis tools. The SNA map is shown in figure 6.6. The network is constituted with 886 nodes and 1926 ties among them. Novartis has formed the largest component and the major actor in collaboration network.

The centrality measures of firms shows that Novartis is the top actor followed by Sanofi, Bristol Myers Squibb, Novo-Nordisk, Merck & Co and so on (Table 6.7). There is not local actor, either firm of other types of actors in the innovation system. The joint patents are mostly from the firms and their various subsidiaries dispersed in various locations. So, it is established from the facts that firms are collaborating among themselves or other types of non-Chinese actors of innovation system.

Table 14. Centrality measure of pharmaceutical firms' collaborative patents in China

ID	Degree	Betweenness	Closeness	Eigenvector
Novartis	201	239788,5	95069	0,699
Sanofi	102	76643,62	95876	0,022
Bristol Myers Squibb	72	112726	95424	0,095
Novo-Nordisk	60	45683,5	96379	0,01
Merck & Co	54	40817,02	96820	0
Wyeth	49	40610,34	96357	0,005

Johnson & Johnson	48	1222	739862	0
GlaxoSmithKline	41	28940,45	96417	0,015
Syngenta	41	27026,55	96103	0,027
Eli Lilly	35	41846,47	96224	0,001
AstraZeneca	30	47246,83	95915	0,008
Alcon Inc.	26	19200	96413	0,008
Sandoz	16	13535,49	96381	0,013

Collaboration network in ICT industry

The following section will deal with the joint patents of firms from India and China. In Inida, among the total 46,474 patents of the total 10 firms there are about 358 patents (less than 1 percent) are joint patents. From China, among the total 123,024 patents, 107, 041 are joint patents (about 87 percent). Therefore, it is clear that firms are doing more collaborative patents from China in ICT industry. The network map is drawn using joint patents as a one-mode network.

ICT firms' joint patent network from India

Similar to the pharmaceutical industry firms, the patent collaboration network of firms are drawn from their collaborative patents (figure 6.7). Patent collaboration of Indian ICT industry has 232 nodes and 185 ties. As described in the table 6.5, among the 10 firms of the sample, Texas instruments does not have any joint patents from India. Samsung Electronics Co Ltd has the maximum number of joint patents from India. A careful look at the joint patents revealed that most of the joint patents of the firms are between their subsidiaries.

Figure 12. Network map of ICT firms' patent network in India

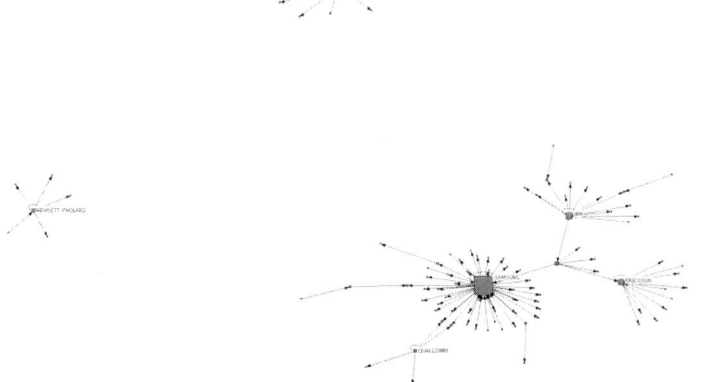

The top 10 collaborating entities in terms of their network centrality measures are presented in table 6.8. Samsung has the highest degree centrality value and the important component in the Network. Microsoft and Intel have very few collaborative patents and the collaboration happens among themselves. Table 8 shows different centrality measures of the actors in the collaboration network.

Table 15. Centrality measure of ICT firms' collaborative patents in India

Sl. No	Id	Degree	Betweenness	Closeness	Eigenvector
1.	Samsung	46	2871.5	35481	0.177
2.	IBM	13	1041	35557	0.006
3.	Ericsson	11	765	35565	0.006
4.	Nokia	9	36	52425	0
5.	Sony Corporation	6	1783	35504	0.164
6.	Hewlett Packard	5	10	53357	0
7.	DuPont de Nemours, Inc.	4	31	52200	0
8.	Pioneer Hibred	4	23	52202	0

	International Inc				
9.	Qualcomm	4	161.5	35631	0.008
10.	The trustees of Princeton university	4	12	53127	0

ICT firms' joint patent network from China

Patent network of ICT firms is quite big and dense and has 1314 nodes and 3450 ties among them. Samsung is the most important actor followed by HP and IBM. These firms are collaborating with various actors and among their different laboratories. Figure 6.8 and table 6.9 shows the network and the famous actors of collaborating patents.

Figure 13. Network map of ICT firms' patent network in China

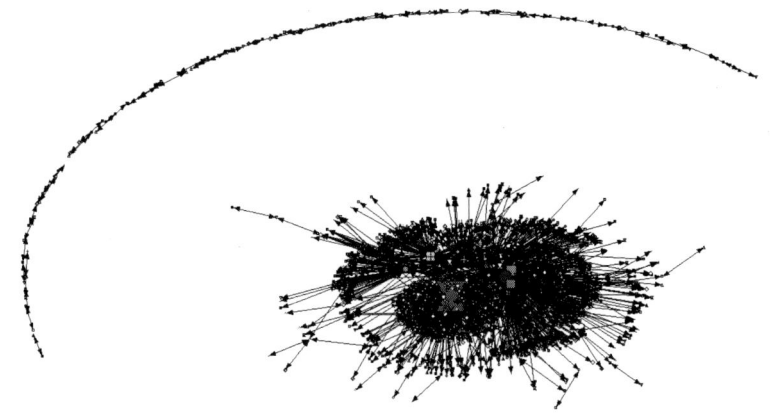

Table 16. Centrality measure of ICT firms' collaborative patents in China

Sl No	Id	Degree	Betweenness	Closeness	Eigenvector
1.	Samsung	403	398798.8	133617	0.635
2.	Hewlett Packard	42	48634.6	134359	0.058
3.	IBM	42	46183.0	134067	0.095
4.	Nokia	40	41823.6	134414	0.058
5.	Intel	35	37849.9	134369	0.057
6.	Ericsson	23	19562.1	134582	0.046
7.	Qualcomm	22	21873.5	134496	0.049

8.	Haier Group Co Ltd	16	12396.9	134365	0.055
9.	Senseage Co Ltd	12	1156.6	135463	0.012
10.	Sony Ericsson	11	9247,2	134652	0,038

In Summary, the firms are increasingly doing patenting and publications from China and India from their R&D centers. However, the number is not much in terms of their global patent portfolio. Firms are collaborating more in China in comparison to India. The collaboration mainly happens with their subsidiaries located in China

Knowledge Spillover

Empirical studies show that spillover happens from FDI in host countries. However, it may be substantially different both within and between industries. However, there is no strong evidence on their exact nature and magnitude. Host country spillovers vary systematically between countries and industries and that the positive effects of FDI are likely to increase with the level of local capability and competition (Blomstro¨m & Kokko 1998). The presence of foreign R&D centers can trigger the spillover effect onto the host country's innovation system depending on the ability, preparedness and policy of the host country (Cohen & Levinthal 1990; Granstand et al., 1999; Mody, 2007; Mrinalini & Wakdikar, 2008). Reddy has categories the potential impact of R&D-related FDI on a developing host country with examples drawn from Indian case. Spillover effects can be broadly classified into *direct effects, spin-off effects* and *spillover effects (*Reddy 2005, 2011). The visible direct effect as categorized by Reddy (2005) is of two types; Technology transfer and sub-contracting R&D to local firms or institutes. The following section gives examples of some selected case of knowledge spillover from the various news sources:

Joint R&D
There are many examples of joint R&D by firms with local entities in China and India. The following section is drawing

some of examples of firms' linkages. Microsoft has signed partnership agreement with 'China Standard Software'. Microsoft has collaborated with this local Chinese firm to develop and market cloud-computing products in China (Microsoft partners with China firm on cloud-computing, 2011). Pharmaceutical firm Bristol-Myers Squibb signed partnership contract with Chinese firms JD Health to establish a comprehensive, technology-driven platform for liver disease patients. Novartis Oncology, Servier China and Pfizer signed their collaboration agreement with Alibaba Health to build an innovative digital healthcare model (Zhou, 2020). Novartis formed collaborative agreement with Chinese biotech company BeiGene to develop Programmed cell death protein 1 (PD-1 inhibitor) for cancer treatment (Zhou, 2020).

There are also many collaborative R&D efforts between a foreign firm and Indian entities. For example, in India Pfizer, signed collaborative agreement with Indian Council of Medical Research (ICMR) to set up a research centre on Antimicrobial Resistance (AMR) in India (ICMR, Pfizer to set up centre to combat Antimicrobial Resistance 2018).

Technology transfer to local firms
MNE's R&D affiliate may transfer few technologies to the local firms developed by them. During the course of R&D, an affiliate may develop some by-products that the MNEs may not want to keep for itself. In such case, an affiliate may transfer such technologies to local firms for commercialization. The following section discusses few examples of technology transfer agreement of foreign firms with local institutes:

- Pharmaceutical contract manufacturer firm Kemwell has set up a R&D facility in Bangalore to cater the need of GlaxoSmithKline's global oral healthcare projects. The facility does development activities, from the technology transfer of the product for manufacture into a GlaxoSmithKline's facility (BS Reporter 2013).
- TCS' has signed deal with Nokia Siemens Networks in 2008.

The deal was significant for TCS for IT service delivery value chain. The deal includes transfer of high-end services such as product engineering, R&D and parts of operations and business software unit's activities from Nokia Siemens Networks to TCS. The deal also includes transfer of 90 employees to TCS (TCS - Nokia Siemens Networks deal, 2011).

- Nokia Siemens Networks has transferred its radio R&D arm in Berlin, Germany, to Wipro Technologies. With this deal, Wipro Technologies enhanced its presence in Europe. About 58 employees of Nokia Siemens was transferred to Wipro Technologies. "This partnership will further strengthen Wipro's capabilities and R&D services in 3G" (Nokia Siemens, Wipro enter deal, 2011).

- Microsoft China R&D cooperates with local companies in four different areas, which include personnel training, software outsourcing, technology transfer, and strategic investment (Microsoft Press Release 10th May 2006).

- Nokia cooperated with about 10 Chinese universities and provided knowledge on Symbian technology through training, seminars and coursework. The transfer of Symbian knowledge was organized with universities of Beijing University of Posts and Telecommunications (BUPT), Tsinghua University, Beihang University, Beijing Institute of Technology (BIT), and Institute of Computing Technology Chinese Academy of Sciences (ICT/CAS). Nokia's R&D facility in Beijing focused on software support and technical expertise in Code-Division Multiple Access (CDMA technology). It also served as a center for technology transfer and local talent development (Nokia Press Release 21st May 2004).

- In 2002, Nokia, Texas Instruments (TI) and 15 other foreign, local Chinese companies and government research institutes have jointly invested 230 million yuan (US$28 million) to form a new joint venture company in Shanghai to be called "Commit" (Jiang, 2002).

R&D sub-contract to local research institutes and firms
A number of firms have conducted joint R&D programs with local firms or institutions. The linkages section has discussed

the issue. In addition, a couple of prominent examples form both India and China are given below:

- MSD India (Merck Sharp & Dohme Corp., a subsidiary of Merck & Co., Inc.) invested about $150 million in setting up a R&D centre at the Jamia Millia Islama, New Delhi in 2012. The facility developed for the vaccine research and drugs for new diseases (Vijay, 2012).

- Agilent Technologies (subsidiary of HP) collaborates with Indian universities for research ideas and to convert those ideas into future market opportunities. The company will focus first with the ideas from leading Indian universities and then will extend its focus to other universities. In this scheme firm will accept doctoral research proposals from students at Indian universities, and will fund and mentor the relevant ideas (Singh, 2008).

- In 2005, Alcatel has signed an agreement with Centre for Development of Telematics (C-DoT) to set up a global research and development centre for broadband wireless products (Galoria, M. 2005).

There are many examples of joint R&D conducted by foreign firms along with the Indian and Chinese entities. The following paragraphs shows some examples of spin-off firms from India. There may be example of spin-off from China, but this chapter is not able to provide that because of the lack of data from China

Emergence of spin-off firms
Technology-based spin-off firms have their initial product idea originated from the previous employment. Such entrepreneurial spin-offs arise when an entrepreneur leaves an organization to start a firm of their own (Dahlstrand, 1997). The knowledge acquired while working in MNEs helps these scientists to set up such new firms. Like labor mobility, knowledge spillover happens when individuals set up new enterprises and exploit knowledge and personal contact gained from previous network.

These spin-off firms do not have direct access to large R&D laboratory but these firms succeed in exploiting the knowledge and personal contact gained from previous R&D laboratories and employees (Huber, 2007). A number of other scientists who worked at AstraZeneca centre have launched startups (Nambiar, 2011; Abrar, 2014). There are many examples of spin off firms from the MNEs affiliates in India. Table 6.10 shows few successful spin-off firms and the parent company they are derived from.

Table 17. Example of spin off firms from foreign R&D centres in India

Spin off firm	Founder's parent company	Year established
Setu Software Systems	Microsoft	2008
Brand Sigma	Yahoo	2011
MindTree	Happiest Minds.	2011
CMS Group of companies	IBM	1976
Ittiam Systems	Texas Instruments	2001
Gangagen	AstraZeneca	2000
XCyton Diagnostics	AstraZeneca	1993
Bangalore Genie	AstraZeneca	1989
EnZene Biosciences Pvt. Ltd.	AstraZeneca	2006
Aristogene Biosciences Pvt. Ltd.	AstraZeneca	2006

Venture capitalists play key role for entrepreneurship not only through their financial support but also through their informal provision of knowledge to the investee company. Venture capitalists have access to wide informal and formal networks of professionals and experts in different firms. This role as knowledge brokers may lead to knowledge spill over. Angel networks like Mumbai Angels and the Indian Angel Network have succeeded in creating confidence among many executives looking for like-minded investors to work with.

Skill and knowledge acquisition by supplier firms
MNEs' R&D activities may ask for new products and services from the local supplier. For satisfying such demands, local firms must have to learn new tools, techniques to meet the MNEs

demand. This perhaps will lead to skill enhancement of local firms on value chain. Table 6.11 gives a few examples of training programs conducted by firms in China in recent years.

Table 18. Examples of training programs by foreign firms in China

Foreign firm	Local entities	Program
Sanofi-Aventis	West China Hospital of Sichuan University	Tied up for comprehensive clinical research & training programs (Sanofi-Aventis and West China Hospital Launch Training Program on Clinical Research, 2009)
Agilent Technologies Inc	Peking University and Shanghai's Fudan University	Opened a semiconductor testing school, which will offer one-year professional training to Chinese engineers. Also, has established cooperative ties with some domestic technology companies and with Peking University and Shanghai's Fudan University in training more semiconductor talents for China (US technology giant to share semiconductor market in China, 2005).
International Business Machines Corporation	Various universities in China	IBM China research laboratory offers various program periodically to transfer the courses to faculty
Nokia	Beijing University of Posts and Telecommunications (BUPT), Tsinghua University, Beihang University, Beijing Institute of Technology (BIT), and Institute of Computing Technology Chinese Academy of Sciences (ICT/CAS).	Cooperation program with Chinese universities, to provide technology transfer in Symbian technology through training, seminars and coursework. The postdoctoral research program to provide R&D opportunities for researchers to work on advanced telecommunication technology research projects at the Nokia Research Center (NRC) in China (Nokia expands R&D in China, 2004). Zhejiang University graduates

		hired for the new R&D centre in China would spend three months training at Nokia head-quarters in Finland (Nokia seeks Hangzhou brains to power R&D centre, 2002).
Cisco	Association of Universities (Colleges) of Applied Science	Training of ICT talent in China, through the Cisco Networking Academy Program, Cisco invested in a four-year program with 100 universities (Paul, 2015).

A number of foreign firms conduct training program in India. Pharmaceutical firms are concentrated on clinical research program. For example, Pfizer offers training programs in clinical research on protocol writing, advanced good clinical practices and all about clinical trials and so on. In IT sector, firms mainly conduct training for their manpower requirement in India. Also, firms like Sun, Agilent offer many training programs of their technologies to the local university students. Table 6.12 gives a few examples of training programs conducted by the foreign firms in India.

Table 19. Examples of training programs by foreign firms in India

Foreign firm	Local partner	Program
Pfizer	Sri Ramachandra University	Joint training programs to conduct clinical research, protocol writing, good clinical practices related to clinical trials. Pfizer provided INR 35 lakh as grant for carrying out these activities in addition to providing training materials and resource persons (Varsity in R&D pact with Pfizer, Business Line, 26th September 2009).

Pfizer	Pharmacy college, Mumbai & SUVEN Pharmaceuticals Ltd	Pfizer along with Pharmacy college, Mumbai & SUVEN Pharmaceuticals Ltd established Academy for Clinical Excellence (ACE). It was the first training center in clinical research established in 2002. ACE provides clinical research education and training for the professionals to design and execute clinical research (The Academy for Clinical Excellence (ACE)
Agilent Technologies India Pvt Ltd	Indian Institute of Science, Bangalore & Society for Innovation & Development	Jointly formed Agilent Measurement Science Center (AMSC) with special focus on scientific research, technology & equipment development and training activities to explore new frontiers in measurement science (India PRwire 2nd April 2009)
Hewlett Packard	Vinayaka Missions University (VMU)	MoU to offer technical and soft skills training to about 2,500 undergraduate students belonging to two engineering colleges of the University (Business Line 20th November 2007).
Intel	NIIT	Launched multi-core training program that would be deployed by NIIT globally to one lakh software developers over the next 3 years (Business Line 27th June 2007)

Summary

This study analyzes trends in foreign firm's external cooperation in R&D based on Biotechnology and ICT companies' newspaper report annual report companies' website and so on. The method called "Literature based alliance counting".

Foreign firms exploiting knowledge globally by increasing overseas R&D centers. The patterns show that foreign firms are strengthening their ties with local firm's universities and public research institutions. The trends are significantly different in India and China. In China, firms are collaborating more with the local universities and research institutions. However, these firms do not regard Indian universities and public research institutions as innovation partners. The University Industry linkage is very strong in India because India has a very strong Biopharmaceutical and ICT sector. Foreign firms are strengthening their ties with universities and public research institutions and systematizing their R&D projects in China. Firms are creating a base at a university and then increase their network throughout the region and country through that university.

CHAPTER VII. DISCUSSION AND CONCLUDING REMARKS

Introduction

The book investigates the impact of globalization of R&D operation of firms in India and China. The book deals with various theoretical aspect of internationalization of R&D and its various aspects. It has also brought various empirical investigations to find the issues related to the globalization of R&D. It is well established in the literature that MNEs are the major deriver of globalization of R&D. In the recent years, MNEs are establishing their R&D units in India and China. The major activities are observed in pharmaceutical and Information and Communication Technology (ICT) industries.

It is discussed in the introduction, that the literature in economics, trade and international relations are very useful in formulating the theoretical framework and research questions. However, much of the approach and perspectives have adopted in the exploration reflected an interdisciplinary perspective. In other words, various concepts and insights in these fields of study are drawn and re-framed within in the perspectives grounded in science and technology policy and innovation studies. However, by no means it is claimed to be a book in economics. This book deals with innovation studies perspectives taking scientometric and social network analysis tools to investigate the phenomenon. However, the fields of economics of technology and technology transfer concerning MNEs have provided useful insights and initial motivation for the study.

This book has explored the recent trends of foreign R&D by firms globally. It further focus particularly on the two emerging economies e.g., India and China. From that whole universe of sample, this study had selected 10 firms from ICT sector, and 10 firms from pharmaceutical sector. To draw a comparative perspective, the firms are selected based on the following criteria. *Firstly,* the firms are big and ranked in the Forbes list. *Secondly,* they have significant operation in India and China, *thirdly* the firm must be doing significant publications and patenting globally and from these two countries, *finally* the firms must have R&D units in both India and China and sufficient information available.

All firms from the sample were from developed countries, with suitable representation from different countries. For example the sample constituted firms from US, UK, Europe, and Korea. The Indian and Chinese firms are not considered for example, Huawei, Wipro etc. The study has further explored the motivations, the innovation potential and linkages of the selected firms and their R&D units in these two-emerging economics. The detail R&D activities (in terms of output indicators) of firms in these two sectors have been analyzed. The study has also explored the linkages of the firms with different actors of innovation system in these two countries. It may be pointed out here that the major findings and conclusions are mainly concerned with the two industries (IT and Pharmaceutical) in India and China. However, the findings and conclusions could not be generalized in the two national contexts. At the same time, it may be pointed out that the findings do indicate a trend that is emerging in these two growing emerging economies.

Major Findings

MNEs play a major role in the world economy and are the main actor of globalization process. FDI is one of the major mechanisms through which MNEs acquire existing assets abroad or set up new wholly owned activities in foreign markets (Narula & Dunning, 1998; Narula & Zanfei, 2005). It is generally assumed that R&D activities by MNEs are less mobile and MNEs prefer to keep crucial R&D activity close to their home base (Mansfield et. al., 1979, Patel & Vega, 1999). In contrast to this proposition, this study has observed that along with the increasing inflow of FDI, many foreign firms have started establishing their R&D units in India and China. At the same time, many have shifted some of their frontline R&D operation in these two countries. Since the last two decades, many firms have started their R&D operations in India and China. Some preliminary evidence shows that foreign firms and doing significant R&D operations in these two countries.

The book explored the motivation of foreign firms to establish R&D units in India and China. A number of 'push' and 'pull' factors (Granstand, et. al 1993; Gerybadze & Reger, 1999) drives usually foreign R&D by MNEs. The factors that influence decisions on the place of R&D depend on a number of motivating factors. The major motives behind the growth of FDI are *market-seeking, resource-seeking* (like skilled manpower at low cost, raw materials, finance, venture capital), *stable investment environment* and to host *government effectiveness* (Gammeltoft 2005; 2006; Thrusby and Thrusby 2006; UNCTAD, 2007).

While in setting R&D units in developing countries, the most important factor is the host country's market size followed by the quality of R&D personnel. Beside these, tax incentives by various host country governments, IPR protection, the expertise of university faculty and so on are also the motivating factors (Le Bas & Sierra, 2002). It is observed that MNEs have established R&D units in India and China not only because of the huge market but also for these countries' knowledge base, skills and human resources. In addition, MNEs' attractions towards India and China are because of strong 'innovation ecosystems. These countries have improved their educational system, which are producing high skilled scientists and engineers. Firms are tapping knowledge from these geographically dispersed knowledge hubs and utilizing this high skilled work force to build their capabilities. This is perhaps the major attractor for foreign firms. Both India and China are promoting 'knowledge parks' or 'knowledge hubs' in many places and sometimes nearby universities (Basant & Chnadra, 2007; Krishna 2012). Foreign firms found the R&D ecosystem of these parks quite favorable to locate their R&D operations. As seen from this study a number of new product announcements, patent, publication came from the R&D units of many global major MNEs like *IBM, Microsoft, Intel, Texas Instruments and so on from their R&D units from India and China.*

In China, market driven motives are the main reasons for firms to do R&D. China is a huge market of 1.3 billion customers. It has a huge middle-class population and their increasing demand (Bruche, 2009). Chinese government has recently started healthcare reforms in the country to provide universal healthcare for its entire citizen. To achieve this goal Chinese government has announced heavy investment in healthcare. These initiatives have created a huge Chinese market in healthcare. Chinese government also opened a number of R&D consortia like *Grid Computing, Cloud computing* etc. To execute these consortia successfully, Chinese government has allowed foreign firms to participate in these consortia. All these initiatives have given tremendous opportunities to foreign firms to exploit their potentials in Chinese market.

The big cities in India (Bangalore, Hyderabad, and Delhi) and China (Beijing, Shanghai) are well equipped with good infrastructure, educational institutions and many knowledge parks. These good and well-established infrastructures have attracted investment. Governments' favorable policies have also definite roles to play in getting new R&D investments in these cities. For example, government of India and China offered

DISCUSSION AND CONCLUDING REMARKS

space to the firms to locate their units in suitable place (for example in knowledge parks, with high-speed connectivity, closer to the universities or research institutes) special tax breaks for firms to conduct R&D operation. Although, government's tax incentive varies according to sectors, it is generally considered as at par with the global standard. For example, government of India gives 150 percent tax rebate to a firm to conduct R&D in India.

MNEs have distributed their innovation activities hierarchically. Advanced technology is usually confined to the advanced industrialized countries. While more routine and low-end innovation decentralized in a few developing countries (Chen, 2008). Until the end of 1990s, offshore R&D by MNEs was mainly to explore new markets. After entering into a new market, MNEs usually developed products to adapt the local market conditions. Usually very little or no R&D conducted in the host country's location. Incremental R&D was mainly conducted to adapt products into the local market condition (Kumar, 1994). Sun et al. (2006) found that majority of foreign R&D centers in Shanghai, did adaptive R&D and tactical in nature. The basic purpose of these R&D centers was to serve the local Chinese market. There were also exceptions, few R&D centers engaged in long-term developmental projects for the global market (Sun et al., 2006). Chen (2008) found that most of the R&D centers in Beijing engaged in basic and advanced applied research. In Indian case, a number of studies have observed that MNE's subsidiaries established R&D units in India were to support local manufacturing operations. However, this study has found a significant change in this paradigm. This paradigm shift perhaps has happened due to the local customers demand and the high skilled low-cost talent available at the host location. Both these two-emerging economics; India and China are huge market and increasing middle class population. To meet these customers' demand as per global standard MNEs need to innovate. In addition, presence of R&D units locally gives customer a kind of 'trust or faith'. Therefore, along with

145

production, R&D activity is also becoming the top most priority for the foreign firms. Beside this, because of high skilled manpower available at low cost in these two countries, MNEs have found R&D operation cost effective and scouted knowledge from these globally dispersed innovation hubs. In this new phase of globalization of R&D, firms have conducted significant R&D in host country's location. This may be termed as a mature phase of internationalization of R&D to more towards 'globalization of R&D'.

Research showed that major reasons for dispersion of MNEs is to secure new technological competencies dispersed globally. A firm's global growth can be considered as a consequence of home based 'ownership advantages' and 'competitive advantage' to be exploited in foreign markets. Offshore R&D by MNEs usually considered being the one of the last corporate functions to internationalize in the value chain (Mansfield, 1975). Firms mainly exploited their R&D strength developed at the home base in the local market of the host country. It can be termed as *"Adaptive Technology"* or *'Home-based exploiting'* (Kuemmerle, 1999). However, present day internationalization strategies of firms deferred from the earlier international strategy of mid to late 20th century. Different empirical findings showed that, until the end of last century, offshoring of R&D was distributed on a triad region (the 'triad' being the US, Western Europe, and Japan). It was considered as a 'regional' phenomenon rather than a true 'global' phenomenon (Rugman & Verbeke, 2003). After that, offshoring of R&D by MNEs had significantly increased. Particularly after 1980's that phenomenon had a significant turn (Niosi, 1999). It is also observed that foreign R&D by MNEs was one way technology transfers from firms headquarter to the foreign location.

Contrary to that, quite a few firms are conducting their crucial R&D away from their home base in the R&D units of India and China for their global product mandate. For example, *Microsoft, IBM, Intel, Samsung* and so on are doing significant

DISCUSSION AND CONCLUDING REMARKS

amount of their R&D from these two countries. In terms of patenting and publication activities (output parameters) used in this study have shown significant increase from both these countries. For example, Korean major *Samsung* have employed about 2,000 engineers in Bangalore R&D unit to develop latest product in mobile technology. There are many other firms like *HP, Intel,* and many others have significant amount of R&D from their Indian R&D units. Empirical evidence from this book have shown that a new trend in the last decade has appeared to be a two-way technology transfer. MNE's R&D units in the new trend have started to undertake *'creative technology'* or *'new technology'* for regional and global markets in addition to adaptive technology for local markets *(Home-based augmenting).*

The empirical evidences have revealed that *in the new trends, that started since the last couple of decades appeared to be a two-way technology transfer. MNE's R&D units in this new trend oriented more towards 'creative technology' or 'new technology' for regional and global markets in addition to adaptive technology for local markets.* However, it may be noted that the result is only indicative trend based on a selected firm. Further study needs to be undertaken to fully understand the nature and characteristics of this trends. It is also observed that a globally dispersed R&D and innovation is gradually emerging.

It is observed that foreign firms in India are working more on global product mandate than the local or regional market. Foreign R&D units in India are working for the new products to sell in the global market. However, many of these units in China are working more towards the product meant for local market conditions. This is because of huge domestic Chinese market, which is a tremendous opportunity of foreign firms to grow.

The evidence of patenting activities (extracted from Patentscope data) of firms in both India and China have indicated that many new patents were granted or filed from both India and China R&D units. This growth of patenting

147

activity has started from the year 2000. This growth curve has taken a momentum after the year 2005. The number of new patents are significantly increased in recent years from both India and China. However, the patents from both India and China are comparatively lower than their global patent landscape. The publication activity of firms (from Scopus database) in both India and China are also increasing. The cumulative number of publications by firms has signified the long-term research plan and investment in 'basic research'. A number of firms for example, *IBM, Microsoft, and Intel* etc. are have published lots of scholarly articles in recent years from their respective R&D units or in collaborations with the entities in these two countries.

In terms of patenting and publications, a couple of firms' orientations is different in these two countries. Few firms are depended more towards India where as a number of firms are relied on Chinese subsidiaries innovation potential to increase their R&D base. Another set of firms are active both in India and in China. For example, *Cisco, Hewlett-Packard, Texas Instruments* are more active in India. *Nokia, Microsoft, Samsung* etc. are more active in China.

Firms' linkages with the local actors have shown different patterns in India and China. In India, linkages are mostly on joint product development program and joint R&D. Firms are involved with a number of human resource development programs. The empirical evidences in this study have found that most of the R&D links are joint R&D programs. The reason for this increasing R&D programs between foreign firms and local entities is because of the recent policy changes. Until the economic transition of the mid-1990s, Chinese public research institutes or universities were the maximum receiver of government grants. However, after the 1990s Chinese academic institutions and government research institutes have optimized the benefit from these resource allocations. As a result, universities and government research institutes have developed healthy collaborations among industries, research institutes and universities on industrial innovation.

In India, foreign firms have preferred industries more than any other entities as their preferable alliance partner. University and government research institute are the less preferable linkage partner for the foreign firms in India. In India foreign firm's collaboration with Indian universities and government research institutes are limited. From a comparative perspective, it is observed that foreign R&D centers in India has interacted more with the private business enterprises. On the contrary, R&D centers in China have a greater number of linkages with universities and the public research institutions.

This book dealt with the 'knowledge spillover' phenomenon from the host countries perspective. Although, it is difficult to measure knowledge spillovers in quantitative terms because of lack of data. There are some findings on this feature. The study has found many examples of technology transfer to local firms, joint R&D with local institutes and some example of spin-off firms. Foreign firms have a number of technology transfer agreements with the local firms or research institute in both India and China. In China, a number of examples are found where firms have technology transfer, training programs with local entities. For example, in the years 2009, *AMD* transferred key x 86 microprocessor technologies to Chinese government to develop its own supercomputing capability. *IBM, Microsoft, Motorola* have a number of university relation program in China to develop human resources. *The above examples have shown that foreign R&D activities generate positive externalities in the host country in terms of backward forward linkages, spin off firms and training.* The foreign R&D by MNEs in these two emerging economics are comparatively new phenomenon. Therefore, there might have comparatively very few examples of spin-off firms by former employees of foreign firms. This study found examples of spin off firms from the former employees of foreign firms in India. However, in Chinese case these kinds of examples are comparatively very rare or may be missed.

Policy recommendations

The literature review and empirical research, which covered various actors and agencies of the national innovation systems in India and China, has thrown up some insights, which may be considered as policy recommendations.

Public R&D expenditure: According to the estimate Indian government, spend about 0.7 percent of national Gross domestic product (GDP) in 2018-19. In monetary term, this is about INR 1,23,847.71 crores. According to National Bureau of Statistics China, it has spent about 2.44 trillion Chinese yuan ($378 billion) in 2020 which is more than 2 percent of DGP. The goal of Indian government to achieve the target of 2 percent of GDP for R&D has not yet been achieved. Although Indian government has committed gross expenditure on research and development (GERD) with infrastructure and sustaining the innovation ecosystem. Given that, these features in turn are dependent on the attraction of FDI in R&D, which is seen to generate a number of positive externalities within the Indian innovation system. The policy signal is quite clear to enhance the R&D/GDP ratio but there is no clear road maps.

Infrastructure in Tier II cities: Today, there is a rapid evolution of a multi-city R&D ecosystem in the country which was earlier concentrated in few Tier I cities. The latter half of last decade has witnessed the entry of Tier II cities into India's R&D map as MNEs have started expanding their network by taking advantage of the higher catchment area, lower attrition, and cost arbitrage benefits offered by these locations. Over 35 percent of the fresh R&D talent pool is now spread across non-conventional R&D locations (Tier II cities) and they account for just below 5 percent of operational R&D workforce. This indicates a good potential for Tier II & Tier III locations. It is evident from the study that foreign firms are increasingly eying to the Tier II cities for setting up their R&D units beside Tier I cities. So, infrastructure and facilities in Tier II cities should be strengthened for a conducive environment for doing R&D.

Industry academia linkage: Industry-academia collaborations play an important role in mechanism for initiating technological or knowledge spillovers. Such information sharing results in technological improvement. It also results in increased patenting, licensing and also spin-out firms. The relationship between the academia and industry should be of interactive, collaborative and participative. Also, the partner should realize and respect each other's role and contribution. Creation of new interface structures such as consortia, partnership research institutions, etc. for basic and applied R&D will strengthen the interface between academia and industry. Public Private Partnership (PPP) could be exploited effectively. Such organizations will enhance the mobility of S&T professionals and promotion of technology transfer and new venture creation. India has a number of this kind of collaborations and government also promotes linkages. This study has found many linkages of foreign firms with Indian universities. However, there is evidence from this study that industry academia linkages are very weak in India in comparison to China. Also, foreign firms collaborating partners are limited to only a few premier educational institutes. Among the academic partners, IITs and IISc are the prominent actors. These collaborations can be extended beyond these premier institutes to other universities and engineering colleges. There are many educational institutes spread across the country which are famous and may have suitable infrastructures which can be utilized to these kinds of collaborations. Particularly the many universities in Tire II cities may be encouraged to extend their collaborations with the foreign firms. Also, India has a very strong network of government research institutes. For example; ICMR, CSIR have a country wide network of excellent laboratories in different fields of science and engineering. These institutes are not that successful in collaborating foreign firms. The potential of these institutes may be used to increase collaborations between government and foreign firms. So, suitable policies should be taken to promote industry academia linkages

Sponsored research: Many scientific developments are directed towards the market characteristics of the intended technology. A market is defined by demand and the demand is dependent on the political, social, economic, cultural, and environmental factors. There may be new technology with either basic or applied aspect may have potential of a project being sponsored by an industrial partner. There is an opportunity for government research labs, universities to grab this opportunity. To build an R&D culture universities and Government research institutes (CSIR labs) should promote faculties or students to conduct joint R&D or sponsored research. There should be suitable government policies to encourage faculties.

Venture capital: Government of India through its various agencies has established a number of innovation schemes for technology transfers. For example, CSIR, DBT, DST has different funding schemes. Recently, through the National Innovation Council, government has proposed to start a venture capital fund for promoting drug discovery. Department of Science and Technology (DST) have many funding programs to foster innovation in biotechnology. Department of Scientific & Industrial Research (DSIR) have R&D sponsoring program. Indian Council for Medical research (ICMR) has many programs which have the potential to translate into the national healthcare program or clinical practice. All these government agencies like CSIR, DBT, DST, and ICMR have filled the gap of VC with some schemes but they should evolve new schemes which stipulate Indian and MNE's ties for new technology development, promotion of 'Spin-Off' firms and the entrepreneurship culture in the country. There are 'Angel Networks' in the country to promote new start-up. These initiatives are expected to provide favorable environment for innovation in the country and to make India an innovation hub. In China, venture capital is comparatively weaker than India. To promote entrepreneurship culture a mature venture capital industry is required.

Education: India has well developed scientific infrastructure with world class educational institutions, like IITs, IISc, NITs and government research institutions, like ICMR, CSIR, etc. India has a strong talent pool which attracts major global major MNEs to set up their R&D base in India. It is evident from this study that MNEs have increased their R&D investment in recent years in India. MNEs like Yahoo! Texas Instruments, Intel, Google, IBM, Motorola, and so on are hiring a significant number of scientist and engineers from India. Both these two high technology sectors of this study have observed this increasing growth of hiring by the major MNEs in India and China. Foreign R&D has tremendous opportunity for new job creation. To grab this opportunity skilled manpower development is required. Education policy with suitable curriculum in engineering and other technical colleges should be developed to produce skilled manpower. So, standard national level curriculums are required to be benefitted from this opportunity. In response, the government has been increasing investment in education and training as a proportion of national income. However, the effort has been inadequate to address the direct needs of the corporate sector. While many employers in both public and private sector invest significantly in the development of their own workforce, they also expect that publicly funded provisions and initiatives meet their requirements.

Suggestion for future research
The study has found that there are many scopes for further research on foreign firms and their potential from both home country and host countries perspective.

Reverse technology transfer: MNEs are the major player in the global innovation activities. MNEs hold and control a large percentage of world's advanced knowledge and technology stock. The decision of a firm to locate their R&D unit in a particular location has great influence on the home country's technological potential and competitiveness. From the developing host countries perspective (India and China), the foreign affiliates are the source of superior technology and knowledge. The intended and unintended spillover from this foreign subsidiary depends upon the readiness of the host country and its institutions including the domestic firm. Also, how much of technology or knowledge is being sourced by these firms from these countries to their home country through "reverse technology transfer" require further in-depth investigation. Reverse technology transfer may also have substantial effects on the firms' home country. There is further scope of research in this aspect, through its linkages with domestic firms requires further investigation.

Government level estimation: There are no uniform estimation of foreign R&D units in both India and China. There are various scholarly works comes in different span of time estimating the number of R&D units in India and China. Different newspaper and popular articles have given different estimation at different span of time. The official Indian Report; *FDI in the R&D Sector: Study for the pattern in 1998-2003* prepared by Technology Information, Forecasting and Assessment Council (TIFAC) covered the MNE R&D activity in India covered six years period. The study has covered a period from 1998 to the year 2003. The report is quite old and there is no estimation of R&D units till date. No new study has come either from India or from China. Foreign Investment promotion Board (FIPB), under the Department of Economic Affairs, Ministry of Finance, and Government of India is responsible for updating the data of FDI. There should have separate department exclusively deal with the FDI in R&D.

There should have separate database fully devoted to FDI in R&D with regular updating and maintenance. Similar responsibility should be shown by the Ministry of Commerce, People's Republic of China

Patent citation analysis uses bibliometric techniques to analyses the wealth of information from patent citation. Patent citations represent a link to previous innovations or pre-existing knowledge upon which the inventions happen. When an inventor cites another patent, this indicates that the knowledge contained in the cited patent has been useful in the development of the citing patent. Patent citation can thus be an indicator of knowledge flows. Patent co-citation analysis has been used to "map" the inter-related development of technical fields. Patent citations are also used to construct technological indicators. Patent citation analysis can provide useful information about the citation patterns of foreign firms. The source they are citing, the important technology, patents and collaboration patterns, science technology linkages. The patent citation analysis will also show from where foreign firms are scouting knowledge. The citation pattern will indicate the relevancy of host country's strength in a particular field. For example; if a firm citing a particular patent, non-patent reference from a source it shows the strength of that particular entity.

More sector inclusion this study is based on the high technology sectors i.e., ICT and healthcare with special reference on biotechnology and pharmaceutical. Both these sectors are high technology sectors and the innovation happens in these two sectors before market demands are created. There are many other sectors for further explorations. For example, consumer discretionary sector (Automobile, Machinery, Consumer Staple (Consumer goods) Industrials (Chemicals etc.) are also attracting significant amount of investment in both India and China in recent years. The overall investigation of these sectors may give a overall picture of the foreign R&D in both India and China. Further, a deeper understanding of foreign firms and their depth of linkages with different actors of innovation system is required. Also, this study is an indicative of the linkages but it requires further investigation of the nature of R&D performed through these linkages. The further study will perhaps be useful to find whether the linkages are for the purpose of adaptive technology or creative technology.

APPENDIX

Appendix I Search string used to search scholarly publications of the respective firms

Forbes Global Rank in 2021	Sl. No	Name of the firm	Search String
		Communications Equipment	
75	1	Cisco Systems, Inc.	(AF-ID ("Cisco Systems" 60030003) OR AF-ID ("Tandberg" 60075160) OR AF-ID ("Cisco Systems Inc., India" 60097543)) AND (EXCLUDE (PUBYEAR, 2021))
709	2	Hewlett Packard Enterprise company	(AF-ID ("Hewlett-Packard Inc." 60020536) OR AF-ID ("Hewlett Packard Laboratories" 60010574) OR AF-ID ("Hewlett Packard Laboratories Bristol" 60110398) OR AF-ID ("Hewlett Packard Enterprise" 60107956) OR AF-ID ("HP Deutschland GmbH" 60107897) OR AF-ID ("Plastics Technology" 60005289) OR AF-ID ("HP Inc. Singapore" 60107886) OR (...) OR AF-ID ("HP Inc. Taiwan" 60107903)) AND (EXCLUDE (PUBYEAR, 2021))
712	3	Nokia Corporation	AF-ID ("Nokia Corporation"

			60026638) OR AF-ID ("G.I.E III-V Lab France" 60108053) OR AF-ID ("Nokia Bell Labs" 60021378) OR AF-ID ("Centre for Discrete Mathematics and Theoretical Computer Science" 60119576) OR AF-ID ("Nokia Denmark AS" 60101003) OR AF-ID ("Nokia GmbH" 60087919) OR AF-ID ("Nokia India Pvt. Ltd." 60081336) OR (...) OR AF-ID ("Nokia USA" 60023290) AND (EXCLUDE (PUBYEAR, 2021))
293	4	Telefonaktiebolaget LM Ericsson	(AF-ID ("Ericsson Sweden" 60016575) OR AF-ID ("Telefonaktiebolaget LM Ericsson" 60004661) OR AF-ID ("Saab AB" 60011728) OR AF-ID ("Ericsson Radio Systems AB" 60000502) OR AF-ID ("Ericsson Inc." 60103834) OR AF-ID ("Ericsson Nikola Tesla d d" 60028968) OR AF-ID ("Ericsson Deutschland" 60075809) OR (...) OR AF-ID ("Ericsson-LG Enterprise Co. Ltd." 60107970)) AND (EXCLUDE (PUBYEAR, 2021))
		Software & Services industry	
59	5	International Business Machines Corporation	(AF-ID ("IBM Thomas J. Watson Research Center" 60017366) OR AF-ID ("International Business Machines" 60021293) OR AF-ID ("IBM Research" 60011048) OR AF-ID ("IBM Research - Almaden" 60009253) OR AF-ID ("IBM Research - Zurich" 60029158) OR AF-ID ("Global Foundries Inc." 60104148) OR AF-ID ("IBM Deutschland GmbH" 60077068) OR (...) OR AF-ID ("IBM România S.R.L." 60108017)) AND (EXCLUDE (PUBYEAR, 2021))
15	6	Microsoft	(AF-ID ("Microsoft Research"

BIBILIOGRAPHY

		Corporation	60021726) OR AF-ID ("Microsoft Corporation" 60026532) OR AF-ID ("Microsoft Research Asia" 60098464) OR AF-ID ("Microsoft Research Cambridge" 60098463) OR AF-ID ("Microsoft Research India" 60098465) OR AF-ID ("New England Research" 60015012) OR AF-ID ("Microsoft Research-Inria Joint Centre" 60170406) OR (...) OR AF-ID ("Microsoft Consulting Services" 60017070))
		Semiconductor equipment industry	
36	7	Intel Corporation	(AF-ID ("Intel Corporation" 60033010) OR AF-ID ("Intel Research Laboratories" 60074754) OR AF-ID ("Intel Development Center Israel" 60102213) OR AF-ID ("Intel Corporation China" 60083495) OR AF-ID ("Intel Technology Malaysia Sdn. Bhd." 60090644) OR AF-ID ("Altera Corporation" 60008002) OR AF-ID ("Intel Technology India Pvt Ltd." 60097645) OR (...) OR AF-ID ("Intel Microelectronics Asia Ltd. Taiwan" 60095829)) AND (EXCLUDE (PUBYEAR , 2021))
206	8	Qualcomm Technologies, Inc.	AF-ID ("Qualcomm Incorporated" 60013301) OR AF-ID ("Digital Fountain Inc" 60102803) OR AF-ID ("NXP Semiconductors" 60027905) OR AF-ID ("Catena Holding B.V." 60114874) OR AF-ID ("NXP Semiconductors Austria GmbH" 60092209) OR AF-ID ("NXP Semiconductors Germany GmbH" 60075813) OR AF-ID ("NXP Semiconductors Philippines Inc." 60089597) OR (...) OR AF-ID ("Systems on Silicon Manufacturing

159

			Co. Pte. Ltd." 60104224) AND (EXCLUDE (PUBYEAR , 2021))
11	9	Samsung Electronics Co Ltd	(AF-ID ("Samsung Electronics Co. Ltd." 60003780) OR AF-ID ("Samsung Electronics Co. Ltd., Russia" 60075515)) AND (EXCLUDE (PUBYEAR , 2021))
341	10	Texas Instruments Incorporated	(AF-ID ("Texas Instruments" 60015272) OR AF-ID ("Texas Instruments India Ltd" 60036281) OR AF-ID ("Texas Instruments Deutschland GmbH" 60098096) OR AF-ID ("Texas Instruments France S.A" 60098093) OR AF-ID ("Sensata Technologies Inc." 60023269) OR AF-ID ("Texas Instruments Belgium" 60098094)) AND (EXCLUDE (PUBYEAR , 2021))
		Pharmaceuticals Sector	
161	1	AstraZeneca AB	(AF-ID ("AstraZeneca" 60004219) OR AF-ID ("AstraZeneca Sweden" 60000666) OR AF-ID ("AstraZeneca R and D Södertälje" 60008043) OR AF-ID ("Sequani Limited" 60172340) OR AF-ID ("Sanatorio Mater Dei" 60024721)) AND (EXCLUDE (PUBYEAR , 2021))
410	2	Bristol Myers Squibb	(AF-ID ("Bristol-Myers Squibb" 60002717) OR AF-ID ("Bristol-Myers Squibb Institute for Medical Research" 60011369) OR AF-ID ("Bristol-Myers Squibb Pharmaceutical Research Institute" 60011480) OR AF-ID ("Bristol-Myers Squibb - Syracuse Facility" 60014178) OR AF-ID ("Bristol-Myers Squibb Research and Development" 60001149) OR AF-ID ("UPSA Laboratoires" 60068955) OR AF-ID ("Bristol-Myers Squibb Canada"

			60083161)) AND (EXCLUDE (PUBYEAR , 2021))
186	3	Eli Lilly & Co.	(AF-ID ("Eli Lilly and Company" 60025685) OR AF-ID ("Lilly Deutschland GmbH" 60072334) OR AF-ID ("Elanco Animal Health" 60031901) OR AF-ID ("Lilly España" 60009732) OR AF-ID ("Eli Lilly Benelux" 60082486) OR AF-ID ("Eli Lilly Australia Pty Ltd." 60084450) OR AF-ID ("Avid Radiopharmaceuticals Inc" 60103337) OR (...) OR AF-ID ("Lilly Ilaç Ticaret Limited Sirketi" 60085897)) AND (EXCLUDE (PUBYEAR , 2021))
97	4	GlaxoSmithKline plc	(AF-ID ("GlaxoSmithKline plc." 60020649) OR AF-ID ("GlaxoSmithKline USA" 60097308) OR AF-ID ("GlaxoSmithKline SpA" 60111447) OR AF-ID ("GlaxoSmithKline Pharmaceuticals SA/NV" 60111446) OR AF-ID ("Glaxosmithkline Biologicals S.A." 60068583) OR AF-ID ("GlaxoSmithKline plc Spain" 60096962) OR AF-ID ("GlaxoSmithKline K.K." 60111450) OR (...) OR AF-ID ("GlaxoSmithKline Ltd Bulgaria" 60111466)) AND (EXCLUDE (PUBYEAR , 2021))
34	5	Johnson & Johnson	(AF-ID ("Janssen Pharmaceutica Headquarters" 60068574) OR AF-ID ("Janssen Research & Development" 60072269) OR AF-ID ("Johnson & Johnson" 60010584) OR AF-ID ("Johnson & Johnson Pharmaceutical Research & Development Raritan" 60026993) OR AF-ID ("R. W. Johnson Pharmaceutical Research Institute" 60018569) OR AF-ID ("Janssen

			Vaccines & Prevention B.V." 60115560) OR AF-ID ("Johnson & Johnson India Ltd" 60079733) OR AF-ID ("Johnson & Johnson India Ltd Ethicon Institute Of Surgical Education" 60079734)) AND (EXCLUDE (PUBYEAR , 2021))
84	6	Merck & Co., Inc.	(AF-ID ("Merck & Co. Inc." 60007995) OR AF-ID ("Merck Frosst" 60020427) OR AF-ID ("Rosetta Inpharmatics LLC" 60014968) OR AF-ID ("GlycoFi Incorporated" 60032403) OR AF-ID ("Merck Research Laboratories Boston" 60031623) OR AF-ID ("Merck Research Laboratories" 60103484)) AND (EXCLUDE (PUBYEAR , 2021))
65	7	Novartis AG	(AF-ID ("Novartis International AG" 60009968) OR AF-ID ("Syngenta International AG" 60017265) OR AF-ID ("ESBATech AG" 60046421) OR AF-ID ("Novartis Institute for Biomedical Research Basel" 60074537)) AND (EXCLUDE (PUBYEAR , 2021))
260	8	Novo Nordisk A/S	(AF-ID ("Novo Nordisk A/S" 60006179) OR AF-ID ("Hagedorn Research Institute" 60012565) OR AF-ID ("Novo Nordisk Ltd" 60107005) OR AF-ID ("Novo Nordisk Pharma AG" 60113568) OR AF-ID ("Novo Nordisk China Pharmaceutical Co. Ltd." 60107003) OR AF-ID ("Novo Nordisk Pharma GmbH" 60107006) OR AF-ID ("BioImage AS" 60083202) OR (...) OR AF-ID ("Novo Nordisk Scandinavia AS" 60080451)) AND (EXCLUDE (PUBYEAR , 2021))
58	9	Pfizer Inc.	(AF-ID ("Pfizer Inc." 60006989) OR AF-ID ("Pfizer Limited UK" 60099418) OR AF-ID ("Pfizer

BIBILIOGRAPHY

			Global Research and Development" 60030796) OR AF-ID ("Pfizer Research Pearl River" 60020915) OR AF-ID ("Zoetis Inc. USA" 60009857) OR AF-ID ("Centro Pfizer-Universidad de Granada-Junta de Andalucía de Genómica e Investigación Oncológica GENYO" 60208599) OR AF-ID ("Agouron Pharmaceuticals Inc." 60006275) OR (...) OR AF-ID ("Pfizer Sweden" 60015996)) AND (EXCLUDE (PUBYEAR , 2021))
72	10	Sanofi S.A.	(AF-ID ("Sanofi S.A." 60010850) OR AF-ID ("Sanofi-Aventis Deutschland GmbH" 60020065) OR AF-ID ("Sanofi Pasteur SA" 60065719)) AND (EXCLUDE (PUBYEAR , 2021))

Appendix II Search string used to search scholarly publications of the respective firm's publications from India

Forbes Global Rank	Sl. No	Name of the firm	Search String
		Communications Equipment	
75	1	Cisco Systems, Inc.	(AF-ID ("Cisco Systems" 60030003) OR AF-ID ("Tandberg" 60075160) OR AF-ID ("Cisco Systems Inc., India" 60097543)) AND (EXCLUDE (PUBYEAR , 2021)) AND (LIMIT-TO (AFFILCOUNTRY , "India"))
709	2	Hewlett Packard Enterprise company	(AF-ID ("Hewlett-Packard Inc." 60020536) OR AF-ID ("Hewlett Packard Laboratories" 60010574) OR AF-ID ("Hewlett Packard Laboratories Bristol" 60110398)

163

			OR AF-ID ("Hewlett Packard Enterprise" 60107956) OR AF-ID ("HP Deutschland GmbH" 60107897) OR AF-ID ("Plastics Technology" 60005289) OR AF-ID ("HP Inc. Singapore" 60107886) OR (...) OR AF-ID ("HP Inc. Taiwan" 60107903)) AND (EXCLUDE (PUBYEAR , 2021)) AND (LIMIT-TO (AFFILCOUNTRY , "India"))
712	3	Nokia Corporation	AF-ID ("Nokia Corporation" 60026638) OR AF-ID ("G.I.E III-V Lab France" 60108053) OR AF-ID ("Nokia Bell Labs" 60021378) OR AF-ID ("Center for Discrete Mathematics and Theoretical Computer Science" 60119576) OR AF-ID ("Nokia Danmark AS" 60101003) OR AF-ID ("Nokia GmbH" 60087919) OR AF-ID ("Nokia India Pvt. Ltd." 60081336) OR (...) OR AF-ID ("Nokia USA" 60023290) AND (EXCLUDE (PUBYEAR , 2021)) AND (LIMIT-TO (AFFILCOUNTRY , "India"))
293	4	Telefonaktiebolaget LM Ericsson	(AF-ID ("Ericsson Sweden" 60016575) OR AF-ID ("Telefonaktiebolaget LM Ericsson" 60004661) OR AF-ID ("Saab AB" 60011728) OR AF-ID ("Ericsson Radio Systems AB" 60000502) OR AF-ID ("Ericsson Inc." 60103834) OR AF-ID ("Ericsson Nikola Tesla d d" 60028968) OR AF-ID ("Ericsson Deutschland" 60075809) OR (...) OR AF-ID ("Ericsson-LG Enterprise Co. Ltd." 60107970)) AND (EXCLUDE (PUBYEAR , 2021)) AND (

BIBILIOGRAPHY

			LIMIT-TO (AFFILCOUNTRY , "India"))
		Software & Services industry	
59	5	International Business Machines Corporation	(AF-ID ("IBM Thomas J. Watson Research Center" 60017366) OR AF-ID ("International Business Machines" 60021293) OR AF-ID ("IBM Research" 60011048) OR AF-ID ("IBM Research - Almaden" 60009253) OR AF-ID ("IBM Research - Zurich" 60029158) OR AF-ID ("Global Foundries Inc." 60104148) OR AF-ID ("IBM Deutschland GmbH" 60077068) OR (...) OR AF-ID ("IBM România S.R.L." 60108017)) AND (EXCLUDE (PUBYEAR , 2021)) AND (LIMIT-TO (AFFILCOUNTRY , "India"))
15	6	Microsoft Corporation	(AF-ID ("Microsoft Research" 60021726) OR AF-ID ("Microsoft Corporation" 60026532) OR AF-ID ("Microsoft Research Asia" 60098464) OR AF-ID ("Microsoft Research Cambridge" 60098463) OR AF-ID ("Microsoft Research India" 60098465) OR AF-ID ("New England Research" 60015012) OR AF-ID ("Microsoft Research-Inria Joint Centre" 60170406) OR (...) OR AF-ID ("Microsoft Consulting Services" 60017070)) AND (LIMIT-TO (AFFILCOUNTRY , "India"))
		Semiconductor equipment industry	
36	7	Intel Corporation	(AF-ID ("Intel Corporation" 60033010) OR AF-ID ("Intel Research Laboratories" 60074754

			) OR AF-ID ("Intel Development Center Israel" 60102213) OR AF-ID ("Intel Corporation China" 60083495) OR AF-ID ("Intel Technology Malaysia Sdn. Bhd." 60090644) OR AF-ID ("Altera Corporation" 60008002) OR AF-ID ("Intel Technology India Pvt Ltd." 60097645) OR (...) OR AF-ID ("Intel Microelectronics Asia Ltd. Taiwan" 60095829)) AND (EXCLUDE (PUBYEAR , 2021)) AND (LIMIT-TO (AFFILCOUNTRY , "India"))
206	8	Qualcomm Technologies, Inc.	AF-ID ("Qualcomm Incorporated" 60013301) OR AF-ID ("Digital Fountain Inc" 60102803) OR AF-ID ("NXP Semiconductors" 60027905) OR AF-ID ("Catena Holding B.V." 60114874) OR AF-ID ("NXP Semiconductors Austria GmbH" 60092209) OR AF-ID ("NXP Semiconductors Germany GmbH" 60075813) OR AF-ID ("NXP Semiconductors Philippines Inc." 60089597) OR (...) OR AF-ID ("Systems on Silicon Manufacturing Co. Pte. Ltd." 60104224) AND (EXCLUDE (PUBYEAR , 2021)) AND (LIMIT-TO (AFFILCOUNTRY , "India"))
11	9	Samsung Electronics Co Ltd	(AF-ID ("Samsung Electronics Co. Ltd." 60003780) OR AF-ID ("Samsung Electronics Co. Ltd., Russia" 60075515)) AND (EXCLUDE (PUBYEAR , 2021)) AND (LIMIT-TO (AFFILCOUNTRY , "India"))
341	10	Texas Instruments Incorporated	(AF-ID ("Texas Instruments" 60015272) OR AF-ID ("Texas Instruments India Ltd" 60036281

BIBILIOGRAPHY

			) OR AF-ID ("Texas Instruments Deutschland GmbH" 60098096) OR AF-ID ("Texas Instruments France S.A" 60098093) OR AF-ID ("Sensata Technologies Inc." 60023269) OR AF-ID ("Texas Instruments Belgium" 60098094)) AND (EXCLUDE (PUBYEAR , 2021)) AND (LIMIT-TO (AFFILCOUNTRY , "India"))
		Pharmaceuticals Sector	
161	1	AstraZeneca AB	(AF-ID ("AstraZeneca" 60004219) OR AF-ID ("AstraZeneca Sweden" 60000666) OR AF-ID ("AstraZeneca R and D Södertälje" 60008043) OR AF-ID ("Sequani Limited" 60172340) OR AF-ID ("Sanatorio Mater Dei" 60024721)) AND (EXCLUDE (PUBYEAR , 2021)) AND (LIMIT-TO (AFFILCOUNTRY , "India"))
410	2	Bristol Myers Squibb	(AF-ID ("Bristol-Myers Squibb" 60002717) OR AF-ID ("Bristol-Myers Squibb Institute for Medical Research" 60011369) OR AF-ID ("Bristol-Myers Squibb Pharmaceutical Research Institute" 60011480) OR AF-ID ("Bristol-Myers Squibb - Syracuse Facility" 60014178) OR AF-ID ("Bristol-Myers Squibb Research and Development" 60001149) OR AF-ID ("UPSA Laboratories" 60068955) OR AF-ID ("Bristol-Myers Squibb Canada" 60083161)) AND (EXCLUDE (PUBYEAR , 2021)) AND (LIMIT-TO (AFFILCOUNTRY , "India"))

167

186	3	Eli Lilly & Co.	(AF-ID ("Eli Lilly and Company" 60025685) OR AF-ID ("Lilly Deutschland GmbH" 60072334) OR AF-ID ("Elanco Animal Health" 60031901) OR AF-ID ("Lilly España" 60009732) OR AF-ID ("Eli Lilly Benelux" 60082486) OR AF-ID ("Eli Lilly Australia Pty Ltd." 60084450) OR AF-ID ("Avid Radiopharmaceuticals Inc" 60103337) OR (...) OR AF-ID ("Lilly Ilaç Ticaret Limited Sirketi" 60085897)) AND (EXCLUDE (PUBYEAR , 2021)) AND (LIMIT-TO (AFFILCOUNTRY , "India"))
97	4	GlaxoSmithKline plc	(AF-ID ("GlaxoSmithKline plc." 60020649) OR AF-ID ("GlaxoSmithKline USA" 60097308) OR AF-ID ("GlaxoSmithKline SpA" 60111447) OR AF-ID ("GlaxoSmithKline Pharmaceuticals SA/NV" 60111446) OR AF-ID ("Glaxosmithkline Biologicals S.A." 60068583) OR AF-ID ("GlaxoSmithKline plc Spain" 60096962) OR AF-ID ("GlaxoSmithKline K.K." 60111450) OR (...) OR AF-ID ("GlaxoSmithKline Ltd Bulgaria" 60111466)) AND (EXCLUDE (PUBYEAR , 2021)) AND (LIMIT-TO (AFFILCOUNTRY , "India"))
34	5	Johnson & Johnson	(AF-ID ("Janssen Pharmaceutica Headquarters" 60068574) OR AF-ID ("Janssen Research & Development" 60072269) OR AF-ID ("Johnson & Johnson" 60010584) OR AF-ID ("Johnson & Johnson Pharmaceutical

BIBILIOGRAPHY

			Research & Development Raritan" 60026993) OR AF-ID ("R. W. Johnson Pharmaceutical Research Institute" 60018569) OR AF-ID ("Janssen Vaccines & Prevention B.V." 60115560) OR AF-ID ("Johnson & Johnson India Ltd" 60079733) OR AF-ID ("Johnson & Johnson India Ltd Ethicon Institute Of Surgical Education" 60079734)) AND (EXCLUDE (PUBYEAR , 2021)) AND (LIMIT-TO (AFFILCOUNTRY , "India"))
84	6	Merck & Co., Inc.	(AF-ID ("Merck & Co. Inc." 60007995) OR AF-ID ("Merck Frosst" 60020427) OR AF-ID ("Rosetta Inpharmatics LLC" 60014968) OR AF-ID ("GlycoFi Incorporated" 60032403) OR AF-ID ("Merck Research Laboratories Boston" 60031623) OR AF-ID ("Merck Research Laboratories" 60103484)) AND (EXCLUDE (PUBYEAR , 2021)) AND (LIMIT-TO (AFFILCOUNTRY , "India"))
65	7	Novartis AG	(AF-ID ("Novartis International AG" 60009968) OR AF-ID ("Syngenta International AG" 60017265) OR AF-ID ("ESBATech AG" 60046421) OR AF-ID ("Novartis Institute for Biomedical Research Basel" 60074537)) AND (EXCLUDE (PUBYEAR , 2021)) AND (LIMIT-TO (AFFILCOUNTRY , "India"))
260	8	Novo Nordisk A/S	(AF-ID ("Novo Nordisk A/S" 60006179) OR AF-ID ("Hagedorn Research Institute" 60012565) OR AF-ID ("Novo Nordisk Ltd" 60107005) OR

169

			AF-ID ("Novo Nordisk Pharma AG" 60113568) OR AF-ID ("Novo Nordisk China Pharmaceutical Co. Ltd." 60107003) OR AF-ID ("Novo Nordisk Pharma GmbH" 60107006) OR AF-ID ("BioImage AS" 60083202) OR (...) OR AF-ID ("Novo Nordisk Scandinavia AS" 60080451)) AND (EXCLUDE (PUBYEAR , 2021)) AND (LIMIT-TO (AFFILCOUNTRY , "India"))
58	9	Pfizer Inc.	(AF-ID ("Pfizer Inc." 60006989) OR AF-ID ("Pfizer Limited UK" 60099418) OR AF-ID ("Pfizer Global Research and Development" 60030796) OR AF-ID ("Pfizer Research Pearl River" 60020915) OR AF-ID ("Zoetis Inc. USA" 60009857) OR AF-ID ("Centro Pfizer-Universidad de Granada-Junta de Andalucía de Genómica e Investigación Oncológica GENYO" 60208599) OR AF-ID ("Agouron Pharmaceuticals Inc." 60006275) OR (...) OR AF-ID ("Pfizer Sweden" 60015996)) AND (EXCLUDE (PUBYEAR , 2021)) AND (LIMIT-TO (AFFILCOUNTRY , "India"))
72	10	Sanofi S.A.	(AF-ID ("Sanofi S.A." 60010850) OR AF-ID ("Sanofi-Aventis Deutschland GmbH" 60020065) OR AF-ID ("Sanofi Pasteur SA" 60065719)) AND (EXCLUDE (PUBYEAR , 2021)) AND (LIMIT-TO (AFFILCOUNTRY , "India"))

Appendix III Search string used to search scholarly publications of the respective firms from China

Forbes Global Rank	Sl. No	Name of the firm	Search String
		Communications Equipment	
75	1	Cisco Systems, Inc.	(AF-ID ("Cisco Systems" 60030003) OR AF-ID ("Tandberg" 60075160) OR AF-ID ("Cisco Systems Inc., India" 60097543)) AND (EXCLUDE (PUBYEAR , 2021)) AND (LIMIT-TO (AFFILCOUNTRY , "China"))
709	2	Hewlett Packard Enterprise company	(AF-ID ("hewlett-packard inc." 60020536) OR AF-ID ("hewlett packard laboratories" 60010574) OR AF-ID ("hewlett packard laboratories bristol" 60110398) OR AF-ID ("hewlett packard enterprise" 60107956) OR AF-ID ("hp deutschland gmbh" 60107897) OR AF-ID ("plastics technology" 60005289) OR AF-ID ("hp inc. singapore" 60107886) OR AF-ID ("hp japan inc." 60107885) OR AF-ID ("hewlett-packard indigo ltd rehovot" 60080388) OR AF-ID ("hewlett-packard brazil" 60104037) OR AF-ID ("hp inc." 60107879) OR AF-ID ("hp inc. united kingdom" 60107893) OR AF-ID ("hp inc. spain" 60107892) OR AF-ID ("hp italy srl" 60107900) OR AF-ID ("hewlett-packard israel" 60080387) OR AF-ID (

171

			"hp inc. france" 60107887) OR AF-ID ("hp inc. china" 60107891) OR AF-ID ("hp inc. poland" 60107894) OR AF-ID ("hp finland oy" 60107898) OR AF-ID ("hp inc. hungary" 60107899) OR AF-ID ("hp inc. taiwan" 60107903)) AND (EXCLUDE (PUBYEAR , 2021)) AND (LIMIT-TO (AFFILCOUNTRY , "china"))
712	3	Nokia Corporation	AF-ID ("Nokia Corporation" 60026638) OR AF-ID ("G.I.E III-V Lab France" 60108053) OR AF-ID ("Nokia Bell Labs" 60021378) OR AF-ID ("Center for Discrete Mathematics and Theoretical Computer Science" 60119576) OR AF-ID ("Nokia Danmark AS" 60101003) OR AF-ID ("Nokia GmbH" 60087919) OR AF-ID ("Nokia India Pvt. Ltd." 60081336) OR (...) OR AF-ID ("Nokia USA" 60023290) AND (EXCLUDE (PUBYEAR , 2021)) AND (LIMIT-TO (AFFILCOUNTRY , "China"))
293	4	Telefonaktiebolaget LM Ericsson	(AF-ID ("Ericsson Sweden" 60016575) OR AF-ID ("Telefonaktiebolaget LM Ericsson" 60004661) OR AF-ID ("Saab AB" 60011728) OR AF-ID ("Ericsson Radio Systems AB" 60000502) OR AF-ID ("Ericsson Inc." 60103834) OR AF-ID ("Ericsson Nikola

			Tesla d d" 60028968) OR AF-ID ("Ericsson Deutschland" 60075809) OR (...) OR AF-ID ("Ericsson-LG Enterprise Co. Ltd." 60107970)) AND (EXCLUDE (PUBYEAR , 2021)) AND (LIMIT-TO (AFFILCOUNTRY , "China"))
		Software & Services industry	
59	5	International Business Machines Corporation	(AF-ID ("IBM Thomas J. Watson Research Center" 60017366) OR AF-ID ("International Business Machines" 60021293) OR AF-ID ("IBM Research" 60011048) OR AF-ID ("IBM Research - Almaden" 60009253) OR AF-ID ("IBM Research - Zurich" 60029158) OR AF-ID ("Global Foundries Inc." 60104148) OR AF-ID ("IBM Deutschland GmbH" 60077068) OR (...) OR AF-ID ("IBM România S.R.L." 60108017)) AND (EXCLUDE (PUBYEAR , 2021)) AND (LIMIT-TO (AFFILCOUNTRY , "China"))
15	6	Microsoft Corporation	(AF-ID ("Microsoft Research" 60021726) OR AF-ID ("Microsoft Corporation" 60026532) OR AF-ID ("Microsoft Research Asia" 60098464) OR AF-ID ("Microsoft Research Cambridge" 60098463) OR AF-ID ("Microsoft Research India"

			60098465) OR AF-ID ("New England Research" 60015012) OR AF-ID ("Microsoft Research-Inria Joint Centre" 60170406) OR (...) OR AF-ID ("Microsoft Consulting Services" 60017070)) AND (LIMIT-TO (AFFILCOUNTRY , "China"))
		Semiconductor equipment industry	
36	7	Intel Corporation	(AF-ID ("Intel Corporation" 60033010) OR AF-ID ("Intel Research Laboratories" 60074754) OR AF-ID ("Intel Development Center Israel" 60102213) OR AF-ID ("Intel Corporation China" 60083495) OR AF-ID ("Intel Technology Malaysia Sdn. Bhd." 60090644) OR AF-ID ("Altera Corporation" 60008002) OR AF-ID ("Intel Technology India Pvt Ltd." 60097645) OR (...) OR AF-ID ("Intel Microelectronics Asia Ltd. Taiwan" 60095829)) AND (EXCLUDE (PUBYEAR , 2021)) AND (LIMIT-TO (AFFILCOUNTRY , "China"))
206	8	Qualcomm Technologies, Inc.	AF-ID ("Qualcomm Incorporated" 60013301) OR AF-ID ("Digital Fountain Inc" 60102803) OR AF-ID ("NXP Semiconductors" 60027905) OR AF-ID ("Catena Holding B.V." 60114874) OR AF-ID ("NXP Semiconductors Austria GmbH" 60092209)

BIBILIOGRAPHY

			OR AF-ID ("NXP Semiconductors Germany GmbH" 60075813) OR AF-ID ("NXP Semiconductors Philippines Inc." 60089597) OR (...) OR AF-ID ("Systems on Silicon Manufacturing Co. Pte. Ltd." 60104224) AND (EXCLUDE (PUBYEAR , 2021)) AND (LIMIT-TO (AFFILCOUNTRY , "China"))
11	9	Samsung Electronics Co Ltd	(AF-ID ("Samsung Electronics Co. Ltd." 60003780) OR AF-ID ("Samsung Electronics Co. Ltd., Russia" 60075515)) AND (EXCLUDE (PUBYEAR , 2021)) AND (LIMIT-TO (AFFILCOUNTRY , "China"))
341	10	Texas Instruments Incorporated	(AF-ID ("Texas Instruments" 60015272) OR AF-ID ("Texas Instruments India Ltd" 60036281) OR AF-ID ("Texas Instruments Deutschland GmbH" 60098096) OR AF-ID ("Texas Instruments France S.A" 60098093) OR AF-ID ("Sensata Technologies Inc." 60023269) OR AF-ID ("Texas Instruments Belgium" 60098094)) AND (EXCLUDE (PUBYEAR , 2021)) AND (LIMIT-TO (AFFILCOUNTRY , "China"))
		Pharmaceuticals sector	
161	1	AstraZeneca AB	(AF-ID ("AstraZeneca" 60004219) OR AF-ID (

175

			"AstraZeneca Sweden" 60000666) OR AF-ID ("AstraZeneca R and D Södertälje" 60008043) OR AF-ID ("Sequani Limited" 60172340) OR AF-ID ("Sanatorio Mater Dei" 60024721)) AND (EXCLUDE (PUBYEAR , 2021)) AND (LIMIT-TO (AFFILCOUNTRY , "China"))
410	2	Bristol Myers Squibb	(AF-ID ("Bristol-Myers Squibb" 60002717) OR AF-ID ("Bristol-Myers Squibb Institute for Medical Research" 60011369) OR AF-ID ("Bristol-Myers Squibb Pharmaceutical Research Institute" 60011480) OR AF-ID ("Bristol-Myers Squibb - Syracuse Facility" 60014178) OR AF-ID ("Bristol-Myers Squibb Research and Development" 60001149) OR AF-ID ("UPSA Laboratories" 60068955) OR AF-ID ("Bristol-Myers Squibb Canada" 60083161)) AND (EXCLUDE (PUBYEAR , 2021)) AND (LIMIT-TO (AFFILCOUNTRY , "China"))
186	3	Eli Lilly & Co.	(AF-ID ("Eli Lilly and Company" 60025685) OR AF-ID ("Lilly Deutschland GmbH" 60072334) OR AF-ID ("Elanco Animal Health" 60031901) OR AF-ID ("Lilly España" 60009732) OR AF-ID ("Eli Lilly Benelux" 60082486) OR

			AF-ID ("Eli Lilly Australia Pty Ltd." 60084450) OR AF-ID ("Avid Radiopharmaceuticals Inc" 60103337) OR (...) OR AF-ID ("Lilly Ilaç Ticaret Limited Sirketi" 60085897)) AND (EXCLUDE (PUBYEAR , 2021)) AND (LIMIT-TO (AFFILCOUNTRY , "China"))
97	4	GlaxoSmithKline plc	(AF-ID ("GlaxoSmithKline plc." 60020649) OR AF-ID ("GlaxoSmithKline USA" 60097308) OR AF-ID ("GlaxoSmithKline SpA" 60111447) OR AF-ID ("GlaxoSmithKline Pharmaceuticals SA/NV" 60111446) OR AF-ID ("Glaxosmithkline Biologicals S.A." 60068583) OR AF-ID ("GlaxoSmithKline plc Spain" 60096962) OR AF-ID ("GlaxoSmithKline K.K." 60111450) OR (...) OR AF-ID ("GlaxoSmithKline Ltd Bulgaria" 60111466)) AND (EXCLUDE (PUBYEAR , 2021)) AND (LIMIT-TO (AFFILCOUNTRY , "China"))
34	5	Johnson & Johnson	(AF-ID ("Janssen Pharmaceutica Headquarters" 60068574) OR AF-ID ("Janssen Research & Development" 60072269) OR AF-ID ("Johnson & Johnson" 60010584) OR AF-ID ("Johnson & Johnson Pharmaceutical Research & Development Raritan"

			60026993) OR AF-ID ("R. W. Johnson Pharmaceutical Research Institute" 60018569) OR AF-ID ("Janssen Vaccines & Prevention B.V." 60115560) OR AF-ID ("Johnson & Johnson India Ltd" 60079733) OR AF-ID ("Johnson & Johnson India Ltd Ethicon Institute Of Surgical Education" 60079734)) AND (EXCLUDE (PUBYEAR , 2021)) AND (LIMIT-TO (AFFILCOUNTRY , "China"))
84	6	Merck & Co., Inc.	(AF-ID ("Merck & Co. Inc." 60007995) OR AF-ID ("Merck Frosst" 60020427) OR AF-ID ("Rosetta Inpharmatics LLC" 60014968) OR AF-ID ("GlycoFi Incorporated" 60032403) OR AF-ID ("Merck Research Laboratories Boston" 60031623) OR AF-ID ("Merck Research Laboratories" 60103484)) AND (EXCLUDE (PUBYEAR , 2021)) AND (LIMIT-TO (AFFILCOUNTRY , "China"))
65	7	Novartis AG	(AF-ID ("Novartis International AG" 60009968) OR AF-ID ("Syngenta International AG" 60017265) OR AF-ID ("ESBATech AG" 60046421) OR AF-ID ("Novartis Institute for Biomedical Research Basel" 60074537)) AND (EXCLUDE (PUBYEAR ,

			2021)) AND (LIMIT-TO (AFFILCOUNTRY , "China"))
260	8	Novo Nordisk A/S	(AF-ID ("Novo Nordisk A/S" 60006179) OR AF-ID ("Hagedorn Research Institute" 60012565) OR AF-ID ("Novo Nordisk Ltd" 60107005) OR AF-ID ("Novo Nordisk Pharma AG" 60113568) OR AF-ID ("Novo Nordisk China Pharmaceutical Co. Ltd." 60107003) OR AF-ID ("Novo Nordisk Pharma GmbH" 60107006) OR AF-ID ("BioImage AS" 60083202) OR (...) OR AF-ID ("Novo Nordisk Scandinavia AS" 60080451)) AND (EXCLUDE (PUBYEAR , 2021)) AND (LIMIT-TO (AFFILCOUNTRY , "China"))
58	9	Pfizer Inc.	(AF-ID ("Pfizer Inc." 60006989) OR AF-ID ("Pfizer Limited UK" 60099418) OR AF-ID ("Pfizer Global Research and Development" 60030796) OR AF-ID ("Pfizer Research Pearl River" 60020915) OR AF-ID ("Zoetis Inc. USA" 60009857) OR AF-ID ("Centro Pfizer-Universidad de Granada-Junta de Andalucía de Genómica e Investigación Oncológica GENYO" 60208599) OR AF-ID ("Agouron Pharmaceuticals Inc." 60006275) OR (...) OR AF-ID ("Pfizer Sweden"

			60015996)) AND (EXCLUDE (PUBYEAR, 2021)) AND (LIMIT-TO (AFFILCOUNTRY , "China"))
72	10	Sanofi S.A.	(AF-ID ("Sanofi S.A." 60010850) OR AF-ID ("Sanofi-Aventis Deutschland GmbH" 60020065) OR AF-ID ("Sanofi Pasteur SA" 60065719)) AND (EXCLUDE (PUBYEAR , 2021)) AND (LIMIT-TO (AFFILCOUNTRY , "China"))

Appendix IV Search string used to search patents of the respective firms

Forbes Global Rank	Sl Number	Name of the firm	Search String
		Communications Equipment	
75	1	Cisco Systems, Inc.	PA:(Cisco OR Tandberg) AND DP: [01.01.1975 TO 31.12.2020]
709	2	Hewlett Packard Enterprise company	PA:(Agilent) OR PA:(Hewlett-Packard) OR PA (Hewlett Packard) AND DP: [01.01.1975 TO 31.12.2020]
712	3	Nokia Corporation	PA:(Nokia) AND DP: [01.01.1975 TO 31.12.2020]
293	4	Telefonaktiebolaget LM Ericsson	PA:(Ericsson) AND DP: [01.01.1975 TO 31.12.2020]
		Software & Services industry	
59	5	International Business Machines Corporation	PA:(International Business Machines OR IBM) and DP: [01.01.1975 TO 31.12.2020]
15	6	Microsoft Corporation	PA:(Microsoft) and DP: [01.01.1975 TO 31.12.2020]
		Semiconductor	

		equipment industry	
36	7	Intel Corporation	PA:(Intel) and DP: [01.01.1975 TO 31.12.2020]
341	8	Qualcomm Technologies, Inc.	PA:(Qualcomm) and DP: [01.01.1975 TO 31.12.2020]
206	9	Samsung Electronics Co Ltd	PA:(Samsung) and DP: [01.01.1975 TO 31.12.2020]
11	10	Texas Instruments Incorporated	PA:(Texas Instruments) AND DP: [01.01.1975 TO 31.12.2020]
		Pharmaceuticals Industry	
161	1	AstraZeneca AB	PA:(AstraZeneca) AND DP: [01.01.1975 TO 31.12.2020]
186	3	Bristol Myers Squibb	PA:(Bristol Myers Squibb) AND DP: [01.01.1975 TO 31.12.2020]
97	4	Eli Lilly & Co.	PA:(Eli Lilly) AND DP: [01.01.1975 TO 31.12.2020]
34	5	GlaxoSmithKline plc	PA:(GlaxoSmithKline) AND DP: [01.01.1975 TO 31.12.2020]
84	6	Johnson & Johnson	PA:(Janssen Pharmaceuticals) OR PA:("Johnson & Johnson") AND DP: [01.01.1975 TO 31.12.2020]
65	7	Merck & Co., Inc.	PA :((Merck & Co.) OR PA:(Schering Plough Corporation)) AND DP: [01.01.1975 TO 31.12.2020]
260	8	Novartis AG	(PA:(Novartis) OR PA:(Sandoz) OR PA:(Syngenta) OR PA:(Alcon)) AND DP: [01.01.1975 TO 31.12.2020]
58	9	Novo Nordisk A/S	PA:(Novo Nordisk) DP: [01.01.1975 TO 31.12.2020]
72	10	Pfizer Inc.	PA:(Pfizer) OR PA:(Pharmacia Corporation) OR PA:(Wyeth) AND DP:([01.01.1975 TO 01.01.2020])
410	2	Sanofi S.A.	PA:(sanofi) AND DP: [01.01.1975 TO 31.12.2020]

BIBLIOGRAPHY

Abrar, P. (2014, February 12). Biotech startups turn chary as AstraZeneca shuts R&D unit, The Economic Times. https://economictimes.indiatimes.com/industry/health care/biotech/biotech-startups-turn-chary-as-astrazeneca-shuts-rd-unit/articleshow/30205031.cms?from=mdr

Academy of Business Studies, New Delhi. 2005. "FDI in the R&D Sector: Study for the pattern in 1998-2003." New Delhi: Technology Information, Forecasting and Assessment Council (TIFAC).

Advinus, Merck establish drug discovery collaboration (2013, February 14) Business Standard https://www.business-standard.com/article/press-releases/advinus-merck-establish-drug-discovery-collaboration-106111601031_1.html

Agilent Technologies announces partnership with Indian Institute of Science. (April 2, 2009). India PRwire. Retrieved from http://www.indiaprwire.com/pressrelease/information-technology/2009040222621.htm

Ahuja, G., 2000, Collaboration networks, structural holes, and innovation: A longitudinal study: Administrative Science Quarterly, v. 45, p. 425-455.

Alcatel, C-DoT join hands for R&D facility. (2005, March 30). Business Line.

http://www.thehindubusinessline.com/todays-paper/alcatel-cdot-join-hands-for-rd-facility/article2173092.ece

Alfaro, L., Rodríguez-Clare, A., Hanson, G. H., & Bravo-Ortega, C. (2004). Multinationals and linkages: an empirical investigation [with Comments]. Economia, 4(2), 113-169.

Almeida, Paul, Jaeyong Song, and Robert M. Grant. 2002. "Are Firms Superior to Alliances and Markets? An Empirical Test of Cross-Border Knowledge Building." Organization Science 13:147-161.

Almeida, Paul, Jaeyong Song, and Robert M. Grant. 2002. "Are Firms Superior to Alliances and Markets? An Empirical Test of Cross-Border Knowledge Building." Organization Science 13:147-161.

Almeida, Paul. 1996. "Knowledge Sourcing by Foreign Multinationals: patent Citation Analysis in the U. S. Semiconductor Industry." Strategic Management Journal, 17:155-165.

Amirapu, D. (2012, May 2) Pharma MNCs GSK, Merck, Pfizer and others prefer tie-ups over acquisitions with Indian firms. The Economic Times https://economictimes.indiatimes.com/industry/healthcare/biotech/pharmaceuticals/pharma-mncs-gsk-merck-pfizer-and-others-prefer-tie-ups-over-acquisitions-with-indian-firms/articleshow/12957367.cms

Andersson, Ulf, and Mats Forsgrent. 1996. "Subsidiary Embeddedness and Control in the Multinational Corporation." International Business Review 5:487-508.

Archibugi, D, and J. Michie. 1995. "Globalization of Technology: A New Taxonomy." Cambridge Journal of Economics 19:121-140.

Archibugi, Daniele, and Carlo Pietrobelli. 2003. "The globalisation of technology and its implications for developing countries Windows of opportunity or further burden?" Technological Forecasting & Social Change 70:861–883.

Archibugi, Daniele, and Simona Iammarino. 1999. "The policy implications of the globalization of innovation." Pp. 242-271 in Innovation Policy in a Global Economy, edited by Archibiugi Daniele, Jeremy Howells, and Jonathan Michie. Cambridge: Cambridge University Press.

Archibugi, Daniele, and Simona Iammarino. 1999. "The policy implications of the globalisation of innovation." Research Policy 28:317-336.

Archibugi, Daniele, Jeremy Howells, and Jonathan Michie. 1999. "Innovation systems and policy in a global economy." in Innovation Policy in a Global Economy, edited by Daniele Archibugi, Jeremy Howells, and Jonathan Michie. Cambridge: Cambridge University Press.

Archibugia, D., and Carlo P., 2003. "The globalisation of technology and its implications for developing countries Windows of opportunity or further burden?" Technological Forecasting & Social Change 70:861–883.

Ariffin, N. 2000. "The Internationalisation of Innovative Capabilities: The Malaysian Electronics Industry." in Unpublished PhD Thesis, SPRU. Brighton: University of Sussex.

Asakawa, K. 2001. "Evolving headquarters-subsidiary dynamics in international R&D: the case of Japanese multinationals." R & D Management 31:1-14.

Asakawa, K., & Som, A. (2008). Internationalization of R&D in China and India: Conventional wisdom versus reality. Asia Pacific Journal of Management, 25(3), 375-394. doi: 10.1007/s10490-007-9082-z

Asakawa, Kazuhiro, and Ashok Som. 2008. "Internationalization of R&D in China and India: Conventional wisdom versus reality." Asia Pacific Journal of Management 25.

Athreye, S., Tuncay-Celikel, A., & Ujjual, V. (2014). Internationalisation of R&D into emerging markets: Fiat's R&D in Brazil, Turkey and India. Long Range Planning, 47(1-2), 100-114. doi: 10.1016/j.lrp.2013.10.003

Aubert, Jean-Eric. 2005. "Promoting Innovation in Developing Countries: A Conceptual Framework." in Report No: WPS 3554. Washington, D.C.: World Bank Policy Research.

Balakrishna, P. , and Sidharth Balakrishna. Aug 06, 2003. "India: The emerging R&D hub." in Hindu Business Line.

Bartlett, Christopher A., and Sumantra Ghoshal. 1989. Managing Across Borders. Boston, Massachusetts: Harvard Business School Press.

Bastian, M., Heymann, S., & Jacomy, M. (2009, March). Gephi: an open source software for exploring and manipulating networks. In Third international AAAI conference on weblogs and social media.

Behrman, I. N., and W. A. Fischer. 1980. Overseas R&D Activities of Transnational Companies. Cambridge, MA: Oelgeschlager, Gunn & Hain.

Behrman, JN, and WA Fischer. 1980. "Overseas R&D activities of transnational companies." International Executive 22:15-17.

Bell, M., & Pavitt, K. (1995). The development of technological capabilities. Trade, technology and international competitiveness, 22(4831), 69-101.

Beryl M. (2014 March 27) Motorola has seen highest sales in its history from Moto G, says Magnus Ahlqvist, Motorola VP DNA https://www.dnaindia.com/business/report-motorola-has-seen-highest-sales-in-its-history-from-moto-g-says-magnus-ahlqvist-motorola-vp-1972513

Bhat, S. (2020). Firm-specific determinants of R&D behaviour of foreign affiliates in India FDI, Technology and Innovation (pp. 145-167).

Blomstro¨m, M., & Kokko, A. (1998). Multinational corporations and spillovers. Journal of Economic Surveys, 2(2), 1-31.

Blomström, Magnus, and Ari Kokko. 1998. "Multinational Corporations and Spillovers." Journal of Economic Surveys 12:247-277.

Boddewyn, Jean J. 1985. "Theories of foreign direct investment and divestment: A classificatory note." Management International Review 25:57-65.

Borgatti, S.P., Everett, M.G. and Freeman, L.C. 2002. Ucinet 6 for Windows: Software for Social Network Analysis. Harvard, MA: Analytic Technologies.

Boutellier, Roman, Oliver Gassmann, and Maximilian von Zedtwitz. 2008. "Foreign R&D in China." in Managing Global Innovation: Uncovering the Secrets of Future Competitiveness. Berlin Heidelberg: Springer.

Bruche, Gert. 2009. "The Emergence of China and India as New Competitors in MNCs' Innovation Networks." Competition & Change 13:267-288.

BS Reporter (2013 January 29) Glaxo expands its R&D base in India. Business Standard. https://www.business-standard.com/article/companies/glaxo-expands-its-r-d-base-in-india-108112101083_1.html

BS Reporter (2013, January 19) Glenmark, Eli Lilly in $350mn licensing deal. Business Standard https://www.business-standard.com/article/companies/glenmark-eli-lilly-in-350mn-licensing-deal-107103000050_1.html

BS Reporter (2013, January 19) Piramal Life starts trial of new diabetes drug. Business Standard https://www.business-standard.com/article/companies/piramal-life-starts-trial-of-new-diabetes-drug-109052000129_1.html

Businesswire India (2008, May 26) GVK BIO enters into drug discovery pact with Wyeth Pharmaceuticals. Financial Express https://www.financialexpress.com/archive/gvk-bio-enters-into-drug-discovery-pact-with-wyeth-pharmaceuticals/314740/

BW Online Bureau (2021, February 10) SRI-Bangalore Completes 25 Years Of R&D In India, Business World. http://www.businessworld.in/article/SRI-Bangalore-Completes-25-Years-of-R-D-In-India/10-02-2021-376027/

Cantwell, J. A., and L. Piscitello. 2000. "Accumulating technological competence: Its changing impact on corporate diversification and internationalization." Industrial and Corporate Change 9:21-51.

Cantwell, John, and Antwell Piscitello. 2005. "Recent Location of Foreign-owned Research and Development Activities by Large Multinational Corporations in the European Regions: The Role of Spillovers and Externalities." Regional Studies 39:1-16.

Caves, Richard E. 2007. Multinational Enterprise and Economic Analysis. Cambridge: Cambridge University Press.

Chaminadea, Cristina, and Jan Vang. 2008. "Globalisation of knowledge production and regional innovation policy: Supporting specialized hubs in the Bangalore software industry." Research Policy 37:1684–1696.

Chen, S. H. 2007. "The national innovation system and foreign R&D: the case of Taiwan." R & D Management 37:441-453.

Chen, Y. C. 2007. "The upgrading of multinational regional innovation networks in China." Asia Pacific Business Review 13:373-403.

Cheng, Joseph L. C., and Douglas S. Bolon. 1993. "The Management of Multinational R&D: A Neglected Topic in International Business Research." Journal of International Business Studies 24:1-18.

Chiarini, T., Caliari, T., Bittencourt, P. F., & Siqueira Rapini, M. (2020). U.S. R&D internationalization in less-developed countries: Determinants and insights from Brazil, China, and India. Review of Development Economics, 24(1), 288-315. doi: 10.1111/rode.12641

Chiesa, Vittorio. 1996. "Managing the Internationalization of R&D Activities." IEEE Transactions on Engineering Management 43:7-23.

Chowdhary, S. (2018, December 26) Bengaluru hub will focus on R&D in AI, Automation, says Sanjeev Tyagi of Ericsson Financial Express https://www.financialexpress.com/industry/bengaluru-hub-will-focus-on-rd-in-ai-automation-says-sanjeev-tyagi-of-ericsson/1424775/

Cisco's China R&D center celebrates 5th anniversary (2010 October 12) http://www.chinadaily.com.cn/business/2010-10/12/content_11401462.htm

Cohen Wesley M., Levinthal Daniel A. 1990. "Absorptive Capacity: A New Perspective on Learning and Innovation." Administrative Science Quarterly 35:128-152.

Dahlman, Carl, and Anuja Utz. 2005. India and the knowledge economy: leveraging strengths and opportunities. Washington, DC: World Bank Institute.

Dahlstrand, Asa Lindholm. 1997. "Growth and inventiveness in technology-based spin-off firms." Research Policy 26:331-334.

Daly, Herman E. 1999. "Globalization versus Internationalization: General Analysis on Globalization." New York: Global Policy Forum. Available on Accessed on 30th November 2010

de Meyer, Arnoud, and Atsuo Mizushima. 1989. "Global R&D management." R&D Management 19:135–146.

Doz, Yves, Keeley Wilson, Steven Veldhoen, Thomas Goldbrunner, and Georg Altmann. 2006. "Innovation: Is Global the Way Forward? A joint study by Booz & Company and INSEAD Survey Results." Pp. 1-13.

189

Fontainebleu France & McLean, Virginia: INSEADand Booz Allen Hamilton.
Dunning, J. H. (1977). Trade, location of economic activity and the MNE: A search for an eclectic approach. In The international allocation of economic activity (pp. 395-418). Palgrave Macmillan, London.
Dunning, John H., and Sarianna M. Lundan. 2009. "The Internationalization of Corporate R&D: A Review of the Evidence and Some Policy Implications for Home Countries." Review of Policy Research 26:13-33.
Duysters, Geert, and Charmianne Lemmens. 2003. "Alliance Group Formation: Enabling and Constraining Effects of Embeddedness and Social Capital in Strategic Technology Alliance Networks." International Studies of Management & Organization 33:49-68.
Edler, J. 2004. "International research strategies of multinational corporations: A German perspective." Technological Forecasting and Social Change 71:599-621.
Edler, J., F. Meyer-Krahmer, and G. Reger. 2002. "Changes in the strategic management of technology: results of a global benchmarking study." R & D Management 32:149-164.
Edwards, Ron. 2002. "FDI: Strategic Issues." in Foreign Direct Investment: Research issues, edited by Bijit Bora. London & New York: Routledge.
Ericsson inaugurates new global services center in Xi'an (2012 October 24) Ericsson inaugurates new global services center in Xi'an. China Daily https://www.chinadaily.com.cn/business/2012-10/24/content_15842695.htm
Ericsson to invest $1bln in China in 5 years (2005 September 07) China Daily http://www.chinadaily.com.cn/english/home/2005-09/07/content_475796.htm
ET Bureau (2009, December 2) Jubilant extends collaboration with Eli Lilly, The Economic Times

https://economictimes.indiatimes.com/industry/health care/biotech/pharmaceuticals/jubilant-extends-collaboration-with-eli-lilly/articleshow/5289635.cms?from=mdr

ET Bureau (2019, December 03) Intel plans to add over 1000 people at new Hyderabad unit, The Economic Times. https://economictimes.indiatimes.com/tech/ites/intel-plans-to-add-over-1000-people-at-new-hyderabad-unit/articleshow/72335638.cms

ET Telecom (2021, May 13) Nokia emerges as top vendor in India's optical network market with over 25% share: Omdia. ET Telcom.com from The Economic Times. https://telecom.economictimes.indiatimes.com/news/nokia-emerges-as-top-vendor-in-indias-optical-network-market-with-over-25-share-omdia/82599994

Eva Dantas (2008, February 14) "The 'system of innovation' approach, and its relevance to developing countries." scidev.net. https://www.scidev.net/global/policy-brief/the-system-of-innovation-approach-and-its-relevanc/

FE Bureau (2021, February 18) Young innovators: SRI-B sets focus on next-gen tech. Financial Express https://www.financialexpress.com/industry/technology/young-innovators-sri-b-sets-focus-on-next-gen-tech/2196871/

FE Online (2021, January 29) Microsoft opens Taj Mahal-inspired India Development Center in Noida, will hire engineers in these areas. Financial Express. https://www.financialexpress.com/industry/technology/microsoft-opens-taj-mahal-inspired-india-development-center-in-noida-will-hire-engineers-in-these-areas/2181389/

Figueiredo, P. N. (2001). Technological learning and competitive performance. Edward Elgar Publishing.

Figueiredo, Paulo N. 2011. "The Role of Dual Embeddedness in the Innovative Performance of MNE Subsidiaries:

Evidence from Brazil." Journal of Management Studies 48:417-440.

Florida, Richard, and Martin Kenney. 1994. "The Globalization of Japanese R&D: The Economic Geography of Japanese R&D Investment in the United States." Economic Geography 70:344-369.

Florida, Richard. 1997. "The globalization of R & D: Results of a survey of foreign-affiliated R&D laboratories in the USA." Research Policy 26:85-103.

Foreign firms hasten R&D establishment in mainland (2006, February 13) China Daily http://www.chinadaily.com.cn/english/cndy/2006-02/13/content_519388.htm

Fors, Gunnar. 1997. "Utilization of R & D Results in the Home and Foreign Plants of Multinationals." The Journal of Industrial Economics 45:341-358.

Freeman, C. 1991. "Network of Innovators: A synthesis of research issues." Research Policy 20:499-514.

Fuller, D. B., Akinwande, A. I., & Sodini, C. G. (2017). The globalization of R&D's implications for technological capabilities in MNC home countries: Semiconductor design offshoring to China and India. Technological Forecasting and Social Change, 120, 14-23.

Gairola, M (2015, April 01) C-DOT, Alcatel to set up R&D venture, The Economic Times. https://economictimes.indiatimes.com/c-dot-alcatel-to-set-up-rd-venture/articleshow/1066484.cms?from=mdr

Gammeltoft, Peter. 2005. "Internationalisation of R&D: Trends, Drivers, and Managerial Challenges." in DRUID Tenth Anniversary Summer Conference 2005 on Dynamics of Industry and Innovation: Organizations, Networks and Systems. Copenhagen, Denmark, June 27-29, 2005.

Gammeltoft, Peter. 2006. "Internationalisation of R&D: trends, drivers and managerial challenges." International Journal of Technology and Globalisation 2:177-199.

Gassler, Helmut, and Brigitte Nones. 2008. "Internationalisation of R&D and embeddedness: the case of Austria." Journal of Technology Transfer 33:407-421.

Gassmann, O., & Han, Z. (2004). Motivations and barriers of foreign R&D activities in China. R and D Management, 34(4), 423-437+ii-iii.

Gassmann, O., & Keupp, M. M. (2008). The internationalisation of Western firms' R&D in China. International Journal of Entrepreneurship and Small Business, 6(4), 536-561.

Gassmann, Oliver, and M von Zedtwitz. 1999. "New concepts and trends in international R&D organization." Research Policy 28:231-250.

Gassmann, Oliver, and Maximilian von Zedtwitz. 2002. "Market versus technology drive in R&D internationalization: four different patterns of managing research and development." Research Policy 31:569-588.

Gerybadze, Alexander, and Guido Reger. 1999. "Globalization of R&D: recent changes in the management of innovation in transnational corporations." Research Policy 28:251–274.

Ghoshal, Sumantra, and Christopher A. Bartlett. 1988. "Creation, adoption, and diffusion of innovations by subsidiaries of multinational corporations." Journal of International Business Studies 19:365-388.

Giroud, Axèle, and Joanna Scott-Kennel. 2009. "MNE linkages in international business: A framework for analysis." International Business Review 18:555-566.

Granovetter, M. S. (1973). The strength of weak ties. American journal of sociology, 78(6), 1360-1380.

Granovetter, M. S., 1973, The Strength of Weak Ties: American Journal of Sociology, v. 78, p. 1360-1380.

Granstand, Ove, Håkanson, Lars and Sjölander, Sören. 1993. "Internationalization of R&D - a survey of some recent research." Research Policy 22:413-415.

Granstrand, O. (1999). Internationalization of corporate R&D: a study of Japanese and Swedish corporations. Research Policy, 28(2-3), 275–302.

Greatwall. 2002. "R&D Yongbao Zhongguo (R&D Embracing China)." Nannin: Guangxi Renmin.

Griliches, Zvi. 1990. "Patent Statistics as Economic Indicators: A Survey." Journal of Economic Literature 28:1661-1707.

GSK strengthens China R&D commitment (2016 October 9th) China Daily https://www.chinadaily.com.cn/business/2016-10/09/content_27000118.htm

Gulati, R. 1998. "Alliances and Network." Strategic Management Journal 19:293-317.

Gulati, R. 1999. "Network Location and Learning: The Influence of Network Resources and Firm Capabilities on Alliance Formation." Strategic Management Journal 20:397-420.

Hagedoorn, J. (2003). Sharing intellectual property rights—an exploratory study of joint patenting amongst companies. Industrial and corporate change, 12(5), 1035-1050.

Hagedoorn, J. 1995. "Strategic technology partnering during the 1980s: trends, networks and corporate patterns in non-core technologies." Research Policy 24:207-231.

Hagedoorn, J., 2002, Inter-firm R&D partnerships: an overview of major trends and patterns since 1960: Research Policy, v. 31, p. 477–492.

Hagedoorn, J., Kranenburg, H. V., & Osborn, R. N. (2003). Joint patenting amongst companies–exploring the effects of inter-firm R&D partnering and experience. Managerial and Decision Economics, 24(2-3), 71-84.

Hagedoorn, John, Albert N. Link, and Nicholas S. Vonortas. 2000. "Research partnerships." Research Policy 29:567-586.

Hagedoorn, John, and Myriam Cloodt. 2003. "Measuring innovative performance: is there an advantage in using multiple indicators?" Research Policy 32:1365–1379.

Håkanson, Lars, and Robert Nobel. 1993. "Determinants of foreign R&D in Swedish multinationals." Research Policy 22:397-411.

Håkanson, Lars, and Robert Nobel. 1993. "Foreign research and development in Swedish multinationals." Research Policy 22:373-396.

Håkanson, Lars, and Udo Zander. 1988. "International management of R&D: The Swedish Experience." R&D Management 18:217-226.

Hakansson, Hakan. 1989. Corporate Technological Behaviour : Co-operation and Network. London and New York: Routledge.

Hansen, Michael W., Torben Pedersen, and Bent Petersen. 2009. "MNC strategies and linkage effects in developing countries." Journal of World Business 44:121–130.

Hegde, D, and D Hicks. 2008. "The maturation of global corporate R&D: Evidence from the activity of U.S. foreign subsidiaries." Research Policy 37:390-406.

Holmes, R. M., Li, H., Hitt, M. A., DeGhetto, K., & Sutton, T. (2016). The Effects of Location and MNC Attributes on MNCs' Establishment of Foreign R&D Centers: Evidence from China. Long Range Planning, 49(5), 594-613. doi: 10.1016/j.lrp.2015.07.001

Hood, N, and Young S. 1982. "US multinational R & D: corporate strategies and policy implications for the UK." Multinational Business 2:10-23.

Howells, J. 1990. "The Internationalization of R & D and the Development of Global Research Networks." Regional Studies 24:495-512.

HP sets sights on China's rural market (2010, December 01) China Daily, http://usa.chinadaily.com.cn/epaper/2010-12/01/content_11637879.htm

HP, Vinayaka Missions tie up. (November 20, 2007). Business Line. http://www.thehindubusinessline.com/todays-paper/tp-economy/hp-vinayaka-missions-tie-up/article1675153.ece

Huber, Franz. 2007. Social Network and Knowledge Spillovers: Networked Knowledge Worker and Localised Knowledge Spillovers. Berlin: Peter Lang.

IANS (2021 February 26) Ericsson extends market share, Nokia faces tough year ET Telcom.Com from Economic Times https://telecom.economictimes.indiatimes.com/news/ericsson-extends-market-share-nokia-faces-tough-year/81231225

IBM to set up centre of excellence for AI with government e-marketplace. (2020, October 05) https://www.livemint.com/companies/news/ibm-to-set-up-centre-of-excellence-for-ai-with-government-e-marketplace-11601914456640.html

IBM, Kingsoft form alliance (2003 November 06) China Daily http://www.chinadaily.com.cn/en/home/2003-11/06/content_278908.htm

ICMR, Pfizer to set up centre to combat Antimicrobial Resistance (2018, January 2031) Business Standard. https://www.business-standard.com/article/news-ians/icmr-pfizer-to-set-up-centre-to-combat-antimicrobial-resistance-118013101308_1.html

Indo-Asian News Service (2019, December 2) Intel Unveils New Design, Engineering Centre in Hyderabad Gadget 360 https://gadgets.ndtv.com/laptops/news/intel-hyderabad-design-engineering-centre-opens-2142150

Inkpen, Andrew C. 1998. "Learning and Knowledge Acquisition through International Strategic Alliances." The Academy of Management Executive 12:69-80.

Inside WIPO https://www.wipo.int/about-wipo/en/

Intel Expands Research and Development in China (2005, September 15), Intel Press release.

https://www.intel.com/pressroom/archive/releases/20 05/20050915corp_b.htm

Intel, NIIT training plan for software developers. (Jun 27, 2007). The Hindu. Retrieved from http://www.hindu.com/2007/06/27/stories/2007062750361600.htm

Iwasa, T., and H. Odagiri. 2004. "Overseas R&D, knowledge sourcing, and patenting: an empirical study of Japanese R&D investment in the US." Research Policy 33:807-828.

Jaffe, Adam B. 1996. "Economic Analysis of Research Spillovers implications for the Advanced Technology Program." USA: Advanced Technology Program, National Institute of Standards and Technology.

Jayaraman, K. S. (1994). India lifts curbs on foreign R and D. Nature, 368(6466), 5. doi: 10.1038/368005c0

Jiang, C. (2002, March 5) Chinese, foreign firms commit to JV. China Daily http://www.chinadaily.com.cn/en/bw/2002-03/05/content_110569.htm

Jizhen, L., & Xin, P. (2006). Globalization and localization of R& D project management process: The culture adaptation of Lucent China Research Technology Center. Paper presented at the Portland International Conference on Management of Engineering and Technology.

Jolly, D., & Masetti-Placci, F. (2016). The winding path for foreign companies: building R&D centers in China. Journal of Business Strategy, 37(2), 3-11. doi: 10.1108/JBS-02-2015-0012

Kafouros, M. I., P. J. Buckley, J. A. Sharp, and C. Q. Wang. 2008. "The role of internationalization in explaining innovation performance." Technovation 28:63-74.

Kaplinsky, Raphael, and Dirk Messner. 2008. "Introduction: The Impact of Asian Drivers on the Developing World." World Development 36:197–209.

Katz, J. S., & Martin, B. R. (1997). What is research collaboration? Research policy, 26(1), 1-18.

Katz, Ralph, Eric S. Rebentisch, and Thomas J. Allen. 1996. "A Study of Technology Transfer in a Multinational Cooperative Joint Venture." IEEE Transactions on Engineering Management 43:97-105.

Kim, C., & Song, J. (2007). Creating new technology through alliances: An empirical investigation of joint patents. Technovation, 27(8), 461-470.

Kleinert, Jörn. 2001. "The Role of Multinational Enterprises in Globalization: An Empirical Overview." in Kiel Working Papers No. 1069.

Kogut, B., and U. Zander. 2003. "Knowledge of the firm and the evolutionary theory of the multinational corporation." Journal of International Business Studies 34:516-529.

Krishna, V. V., Patra, S. K., & Bhattacharya, S. (2012). Internationalisation of R&D and global nature of innovation: Emerging trends in India. Science, Technology and Society, 17(2), 165-199.

Kuemmerle, Walter. 1999. "Foreign direct investment in industrial research in the pharmaceutical and electronics industries—results from a survey of multinational firms." Research Policy 28:179-193.

Lall, S. (1992). Technological capabilities and industrialization. World development, 20(2), 165-186.

Lall, Sanjaya. 2003. "Foreign direct investment, technology development and competitiveness: issues and evidence." Pp. 12-56 in Competitiveness, FDI and Technological Activity in East Asia, edited by Lall Sanjaya and Urata Shujiro. Cheltenham: Edward Elgar.

Le Bas, C., and C. Sierra. 2002. "Location versus home country advantages' in R&D activities: some further results on multinationals' locational strategies." Research Policy 31:589-609.

Leslie D'Monte (2017, January 03) Mint https://www.livemint.com/Industry/Lg4vwrrO1tyS3BfaELvNAI/India-an-innovation-hub-for-Microsoft.html

Li Weitao (2006 May 24) Nokia to build new China hub. China Daily. http://www.chinadaily.com.cn/bizchina/2006-05/24/content_598824.htm

Li Weitao (2006, March 25) Motorola launches another R&D centre, China Daily

Li Weitao (2006, March 25) Motorola launches another R&D centre, China Daily http://www.chinadaily.com.cn/cndy/2006-03/25/content_551932.htm

Li, W (2005, October 13) Cisco opens research facility in Shanghai. China Daily http://www.chinadaily.com.cn/english/cndy/2005-10/13/content_484485.htm

Li, W (2015, October 13) Cisco opens research facility in Shanghai. China Daily http://www.chinadaily.com.cn/english/cndy/2005-10/13/content_484485.htm

Li, W. (2006, May 13) HP to hire 1,000 in recruitment drive. China Daily http://www.chinadaily.com.cn/cndy/2006-05/13/content_588925.htm

Little, Arthur, D., and R. Veugelers. 2005. "Internationalization of R&D in the UK : A review of the evidence." Cambridge: The Office of Science and Technology.

Liu Zheng (2015 September 27) Ericsson aims big in China market: top executive. http://europe.chinadaily.com.cn/business/2015-09/27/content_21994270.htm

Liu, B., (2005 June 29) Microsoft joins forces with Amoi China Daily http://www.chinadaily.com.cn/english/cndy/2005-06/29/content_455412.htm

Liu, Q., Guo, P., Lei, Y., & Feng, Y. (2018). Research on foreign capital R&D ecosystem in China based on dissipative structure theory. Paper presented at the IEEE International Conference on Industrial Engineering and Engineering Management.

Lundin, Nannan, Sylvia Schwaag Serger, Martin Berger, Lan Xue, and Zheng Liang. 2008. "China and the Globalization of Research and Development." Pp. 263-304 in OECD Reviews of Innovation Policy, China. Paris: Organization for Economic Cooperation and Development.

Lundvall, Bengt-Ake. 2008. "Preface." International Journal of Technology and Globalization 4:1-4.

Ma, S. (2020 July 30) Qualcomm, Huawei sign patent licensing deal. China Daily https://www.chinadaily.com.cn/a/202007/30/WS5f22 5f1ea31083481725d248.html

Mansfield, E., D. Teece, and A. Romeo. 1979. "Overseas research and development by U.S. based firms." Economica 46:187–196.

Mansfield, Edwin. 1975. "International Technology Transfer: Forms, Resource Requirements, and Policies." The American Economic Review 65:372-376.

Marshall, A. (2009). Principles of economics: unabridged eighth edition. Cosimo, Inc..

Melin, G., & Persson, O. (1996). Studying research collaboration using co-authorships. Scientometrics, 36(3), 363-377.

Merton, R. K. (1957). Priorities in scientific discovery: a chapter in the sociology of science. American sociological review, 22(6), 635-659.

Meyer-Krahmer, Frieder, and Guido Reger. 1999. "New perspectives on the innovation strategies of multinational enterprises: lessons for technology policy in Europe." Research Policy 28:751–776.

Microsoft partners with China firm on cloud-computing (2011 August 23) China Daily http://usa.chinadaily.com.cn/business/2011-08/23/content_13174397.htm

Miyazaki, K., & Ying, H. (2009). An empirical study of the R&D globalization of japanese firms towards China. Paper presented at the PICMET: Portland International Center for Management of Engineering and Technology, Proceedings.

Mody, A. (2007). Is FDI integrating the world economy? In A. Mody (Ed.), Foreign Direct Investment and the World Economy. New York: Routlegde.

Mody, Ashoka. 2007. "Is FDI integrating the world economy?" in Foreign Direct Investment and the World Economy, edited by Ashoka Mody. New York: Routlegde.

Mohd U. (2018, July 02) Challenge posed by India offers huge opportunity for Cisco to grow globally: Cisco MD Sanjay Kaul. https://www.financialexpress.com/industry/challenge-posed-by-india-offers-huge-opportunity-for-cisco-to-grow-globally-cisco-md-sanjay-kaul/1227828/

Motohashi, Kazuyuki. 2005. "R&D of Multinationals in China: Structure, Motivations and Regional Difference." RIETI Discussion Paper Series 06-E-005.

Motohashi, Kazuyuki. 2010. "R&D Activities of Manufacturing Multinationals in China: Structure, Motivations and Regional Differences." China & World Economy 18:56-72.

Motorola opens new R&D centre (2006 September 14) China Daily http://www.chinadaily.com.cn/bizchina/2006-09/14/content_688545.htm

Motorola opens new R&D centre (2006, September 14) China Daily http://www.chinadaily.com.cn/bizchina/2006-09/14/content_688545.htm

Mrinalini, N. 2009. "Changing innovation dynamics in India: the role of foreign direct investment in research and development activities." Int. J. Indian Culture and Business Management 2:95-110.

Mrinalini, N., and S Wakdikar. 2008. "Foreign R&D centres in India: Is there any positive impact?" Current Science 94:452-458.

Mrinalini, N., Nath, P., & Sandhya, G. D. (2013). Foreign direct investment in R&D in India. Current Science, 105(6), 767-773.

Nagaoka, Sadao, Kazuyuki Motohashi, and Akira Goto. 2010. "Patent Statistics as an Innovation Indicator" Pp. 1083-1127 in Handbook of the Economics of Innovation, Volume 2, edited by Bronwyn H. Hall and Nathan Rosenberg: North-Holland.

Nagpal, Aditi. 2010. "Caps are good, but then caps limit R&D." in Financial Express. New Delhi.

Nakamura, Masao. 2003. "Research Alliances and Collaborations: Introduction to the Special Issue." Managerial and Decision Economics 24:47-49.

Nambiar, P. (2011, November 12). BrandSigma: Former Yahoo executive, Sharad Sharma, joins list of tech veterans in startup mode, The Economic Times. https://economictimes.indiatimes.com/news/company/corporate-trends/brandsigma-former-yahoo-executive-sharad-sharma-joins-list-of-tech-veterans-in-startup-mode/articleshow/10701325.cms

Narula, R, and G Duysters. 2004. "Globalisation and trends in international R&D alliances." Journal of International Management 10:199-218.

Narula, R. 2003. Globalisation and Technology: Interdependence, Innovation Systems and Industrial Policy. Cambridge: Polity Press.

Narula, R., and J.H. Dunning. 1998. "Explaining international R&D alliances and the role of governments." International Business Review 7:377-397.

Narula, R; Zanfei, A. 2005. "Globalisation of Innovation: The Role of Multinational Enterprises." in Handbook of Innovation, edited by David Mowery Jan Fagerberg, and Richard R. Nelson. Oxford: Oxford University Press.

Narula, Rajneesh. 2003. Globalisation and Technology. Cambridge: Polity Press.

Narula, Rajneesh. 24-26 January 2005. "Knowledge creation and why it matters for development: the role of TNCs." in Globalization of R&D and Developing Countries: Proceedings of the Expert Meeting. Geneva: United Nations Conference on Trade and Development.

National Science Foundation. 1990. "Research and development in industry." Washington, D.C.: National Science Foundation.

Newman, M. (2018). Networks. Oxford university press.

Nicholas, Stephen and Maitland, Elizabeth. 2002. "International business research: steady-states, dynamics and globalization." Pp. 7-27 in Foreign Direct Investment: Research Issues, edited by Bijit Bora. London & New York: Routledge.

Niosi, J. 1999. "The Internationalization of Industrial R&D From technology transfer to the learning organization." Research Policy 28:107-117.

Niosi, J. and Benoit G. 1999. "Canadian R&D abroad management practices." Research Policy 23:215-230.

Nobel, R., and Julian B. 1998. "Innovation in Multinational Corporations: Control and Communication Patterns in International R&D Operations." Strategic Management Journal 19:479-496.

Nobelius, D. 2004. "Towards the sixth generation of R&D management." International Journal of Project Managemen 22:369-375.

Nokia expands R&D in China. (2004, May 26). EETAsia. http://www.eetasia.com/ART_8800337596_590626_N T_393ec50d.HTM

Nokia Expands Research and Development in China. (May 21, 2004), from http://press.nokia.com/2004/05/21/nokia-expands-research-and-development-in-china/

Nokia seeks Hangzhou brains to power R&D centre. (2002 January 11), C114 http://www.cn-c114.net/582/a299837.html

Nokia Siemens, Wipro enter deal. (2011 April 9). Business Line. http://www.thehindubusinessline.com/todays-paper/tp-info-tech/nokia-siemens-wipro-enter-deal/article1671797.ece

Odagiri, H., and H. Yasuda. 1996. "The determinants of overseas R&D by Japanese firms: An empirical study at the industry and company levels." Research Policy 25:1059-1079.

OECD Handbook on Economic Globalization Indicators: OECD: Organization for Economic Co-operation and Development, 2005

OECD. 2008. "The Internationalization of Business R&D : Evidence, Impact and implications." Paris: Organization for Economic Co-Operation and Development (OECD).

Ohmae, Kenichi. 1999. The Borderless World: Power and Strategy in the Interlinked Economy. New York: HarperCollins Publishers.

Patel, P, and M Vega. 1999. "Patterns of internationalization of corporate technology: location vs. home country advantages." Research Policy 28:145-155.

Patel, P., and K. Pavitt. 1991. "Large Firms in the Production of the World's Technology: An Important Case of "Non-globalization "." Journal of International Business Studies 22:1-21.

Patra, S. K. (2017). Foreign R&D units in India and China: An empirical exploration. African Journal of Science, Technology, Innovation and Development, 9(5), 557-571.

Patra, S. K., & Krishna, V. V. (2015). Globalization of R &D and open innovation: Linkages of foreign R&D centers in India. Journal of Open Innovation: Technology, Market, and Complexity, 1(1).

Patra, S. K. (2012). Internationalization of R&D: A Study of foreign ICT and Biotechnology firms in India and China (Unpublished doctoral dissertation), Centre for Studies in Science Policy, Jawaharlal Nehru University, New Delhi, India

Patra, S. K. (2014). Innovation Network in IT Sector: A study of Collaboration patterns among selected foreign IT firms in India and China. In Collaboration in International and Comparative Librarianship (pp. 148-170). IGI Global.

Paul (2015, June 23) Cisco $10b investment to revive China business China Daily http://usa.chinadaily.com.cn/epaper/2015-06/23/content_21077937.htm

Pavitt, K. 1985. "Patent Statistics as Indicators of Innovative Activities: Possibilities and Problems." Seientometrics 7:77-99.

Pavitt, K., and P Patel. 1999. "Global Corporations and National Systems of Innovation: Who Dominates Whom?" in Innovation Policy in a Global Economy, edited by Archibiugi Daniele, Jeremy Howells, and Jonathan Michie. Cambridge: Cambridge University Press.

Pearce, R. D. 1989. The Internationalization of Research and Development by Multinational Enterprises. New York: St. Martin's Press.

Pearce, R., and M Papanastassiou. 1999. "Overseas R & D and the strategic evolution of MNEs: evidence from laboratories in the UK." Research Policy 28:23-41.

Pearce, Robert, and Marina Papanastassiou. 1996. "R&D networks and innovation: decentralized product development in multinational enterprises." R&D Management 26:315-333.

Pearce, Robert. 1994. "The Internationalisation of Research and Development by Multinational Enterprises and the Transfer Sciences." Empiriea 21:297-311.

Pearce, Robert. 1997. "The Implication for Host-Country Competitiveness of the Internationalization of R&D and Innovation in Multinationals." Pp. 13-50 in Global Competition and Technology: Essays in the Creation and Application of Knowledge by Multinationals, edited by Pearce Robert. New York: St. Martin's Press.

Pearce, Robert. 1999. "The evolution of technology in multinational enterprises: the role of creative subsidiaries." International Business Review 8:125–148.

Pfizer (2011, June 1) Pfizer and Hisun sign MoU to increase access to quality and low-cost medicines for patients in China https://www.pfizer.com/news/press-release/press-release-detail/pfizer_and_hisun_sign_mou_to_increase_access_to_quality_and_low_cost_medicines_for_patients_in_china

Pfizer (2011, September 8) Pfizer And Guoyuan Form Joint Venture To Expand Development, Manufacture And Distribution Of Animal Vaccines In China https://www.pfizer.com/news/press-release/press-release-detail/pfizer_and_guoyuan_form_joint_venture_to_expand_development_manufacture_and_distribution_of_animal_vaccines_in_china

PharmaTimes (2007, November 20) Merck & Co in oncology R&D pact with Nicholas Piramal, PharmaTimes Online http://www.pharmatimes.com/news/merck_and_co_in_oncology_r_and_d_pact_with_nicholas_piramal_991414

Porter, M. E. (1990). The competitive advantage of nations. Competitive Intelligence Review, 1(1), 14-14.

Powell, W. W., and G. Stine, 2006, Networks of Innovators, in D. M. Jan Fagerberg, and Richard R. Nelson, ed., The Oxford Handbook of Innovation: Oxford, Oxford University Press, p. 56-85.

Pramanik, A (2019, March 5) Hewlett Packard Enterprise storage unit growth beats data centre's in India. The Economic Times. https://economictimes.indiatimes.com/tech/ites/hewlett-packard-enterprise-storage-unit-growth-beats-data-centres-in-india/articleshow/68263266.cms

Prater, Edmund, and Bin Jiang. 2008. "The Drivers of Foreign R&D Investment in China." Journal of Marketing Channels 15:211 - 233.

PTI (2020, February 18) Microsoft Sets Up R&D Centre in Noida, Its Third Such Facility in India. Firstspot. https://www.firstpost.com/tech/news-analysis/microsoft-sets-up-rd-centre-in-noida-its-third-such-facility-in-india-8054511.html

PTI (2020, March 03) Cisco says India highest growing country in APJC region. ET Telcom.com from The Economic Times. https://telecom.economictimes.indiatimes.com/news/cisco-says-india-highest-growing-country-in-apjc-region/74450794

Pulakat, H. (2011, Dec 30) India will be a centre of frugal engineering in year 2012, The Economics Times https://economictimes.indiatimes.com/news/company/corporate-trends/india-will-be-a-centre-of-frugal-engineering-in-year-2012/articleshow/11291974.cms

R&D in India: The Curtain Rises, The Play Has Begun… November 21, 2005. Knowledge@Wharton.

Ranbaxy, GSK Enter New R&D Pact (2007, July 2) Contract Pharma https://www.contractpharma.com/contents/view_breaking-news/2007-02-07/ranbaxy-gsk-enter-new-r-amp-d-pact

Reddy, N. Mohan, and Liming ZHAO. 1990. "International technology transfer: A review." Research Policy 19:285-307.

Reddy, P. (1997). New trends in globalization of corporate R&D and implications for innovation capability in host countries: a survey from India. World development, 25(11), 1821-1837.

Reddy, P. (2000). The globalization of corporate R & D: Implications for innovation systems in host countries. Routledge.

Reddy, P. (2005). R&D-related FDI in developing countries: implications for host countries Globalization of R&D and Developing Countries: Proceedings of the Expert Meeting Geneva 24-26 January 2005. Geneva: United Nations.

Reddy, P. (2011). Global Innovation in Emerging Economies. New York: Routledge.

Reddy, P. 2005. "R&D-related FDI in developing countries: implications for host countries." in Globalization of R&D and Developing Countries: Proceedings of the Expert Meeting Geneva 24-26 January 2005. Geneva: United Nations United Nations Conference on Trade and Development (UNCTAD).

Reddy, P., & Sigurdson, J. (1997). Strategic location of R&D and emerging patterns of globalization: The case of Astra Research Centre India. International Journal of Technology Management, 14(2-4), 344-361.

Ren, S., & Su, P. (2015). Open innovation and intellectual property strategy: the catch-up processes of two Chinese pharmaceutical firms. Technology Analysis & Strategic Management, 27(10), 1159-1175.

Report of the Steering Group on Foreign Direct Investment. New Delhi: Planning Commission, Government of India, August 2002.

Ronstadt, R. 1977. Research and Development Abroad by U.S. Multinationals. New York: Praeger.

Rugman, Alan, and Alain Verbeke. 2003. "Regional Multinationals: The Location-bound Drivers of Global Strategy." Pp. 45-57 in The Future of the Multinational

Company, edited by Sumantra Ghoshal Julian Birkinshaw, Constantinos Markides, John Stopford, George Yip. West Sussex, England: John Wiley & Sons Ltd.

Ruzzier Mitja, Hisrich Robert D, and Antoncic Bostjan. 2006. "SME internationalization research: past, present, and future." Journal of Small Business and Enterprise Development 13:476-497.

Sachwald, Fre´de´rique. 2008. "Location choices within global innovation networks: the case of Europe." Journal of Technology Transfer 33:364-378.

Saliola, Federica, and Antonello Zanfei. 2009. "Multinational firms, global value chains and the organization of knowledge transfer." Research Policy 38:369–381.

Sanofi-Aventis and West China Hospital Launch Training Program on Clinical Research. (2009, October 20,). Pharm Asia News, from http://www.pharmamedtechbi.com/publications/pharmasia-news/2009/10/20/sanofiaventis-and-west-china-hospital-launch-training-program-on-clinical-research

Satyanand, Premila Nazareth. October 1, 2007. "Regions: Asia - Chemical attraction." in FT Business.

Schweizer, R., Lagerström, K., & Jakobsson, J. (2020). The evolution of MNCs' R&D foreign units: the case of Swedish MNCs in India. Cross Cultural and Strategic Management, 27(3), 365-388. doi: 10.1108/CCSM-06-2019-0116

Scopus Content Coverage Guide (2020) available at: https://www.elsevier.com/__data/assets/pdf_file/0007/69451/Scopus_ContentCoverage_Guide_WEB.pdf accessed on 30th June 2021

Scott, J., & Stokman, F. N. (2015). Social Networks. In J. D. Wright (Ed.), International Encyclopedia of the Social & Behavioral Sciences (Second Edition) (pp. 473-477). Oxford: Elsevier.

Sharma, A., Chakki, N & Varmani, M. (2020, October 29) The Case for Foreign Direct Investment in Research & Development in India, Invest India https://www.investindia.gov.in/siru/case-foreign-direct-investment-research-development-india

Shen, J. (2013 September 25) Microsoft and BesTV alliance is a good sign. China Daily http://www.chinadaily.com.cn/business/tech/2013-09/25/content_16992270.htm

Shimizutani, S., and and Y. Todo. 2008. "What determines overseas R&D activities? The case of Japanese multinational firms." Research Policy 37:530-544.

Siddharthan, N. S., and K. Narayanan, 2010, Introduction, in N. S. Siddharthan, and K. Narayanan, eds., Indian and Chinese Enterprises: Global trade, technology and investment regimes: London, Routledge, p. 1-34.

Singh, S. (2008 April 24). Agilent arm to scour Indian tech institutes for research ideas, Live Mint. http://www.livemint.com/Industry/FHF3KHjfdALHgBCeFCiInI/Agilent-arm-to-scour-Indian-tech-institutes-for-research-ide.html

Singh, S. (2010, September 3), Texas Instruments: Growth with work centering around low cost innovation. The Economic Times https://economictimes.indiatimes.com/texas-instruments-growth-with-work-centering-around-low-cost-innovation/articleshow/6482066.cms

Sooreea, R., Damodar, S., Sharma, S., & Sooreea-Bheemul, B. (2018). How attractive is India to foreign R&D-based biotech businesses? U.S. Micro-multinational enterprises. SCMS Journal of Indian Management, 15(4), 12-21.

Steketee, M., Miyaoka, A., & Spiegelman, M. (2015). Social Network Analysis. In J. D. Wright (Ed.), International Encyclopedia of the Social & Behavioral Sciences (Second Edition) (pp. 461-467). Oxford: Elsevier.

Stiglitz, Joseph E. 2002. Globalization and Its Discontents. New York: Norton & Company.
Strategic Partnership Group. from http://www.microsoft.com/china/ard/spg/en/default.mspx
Suarez-Villa, Luis. 2002. "Networked Alliances and Innovation." in The Emergence of the Knowledge Economy: A Regional Perspective, edited by Zoltan J. Acs, Henri L.F. de Groot, and Peter Nijkamp. New York: Springer.
Sun, Y. F., and Ke Wen. 2007. "Uncertainties, Imitative Behaviours and Foreign R&D Location: Explaining the Over-concentration of Foreign R&D in Beijing and Shanghai within China." Asia Pacific Business Review 13:405-424.
Sun, Y. F., D. B. Du, and L. Huang. 2006. "Foreign R & D in developing countries: Empirical evidence from Shanghai, China." China Review-an Interdisciplinary Journal on Greater China 6:67-91.
Sun, Y., & Wen, K. (2007). Country relational distance, organizational power and R&D managers: Understanding environmental challenges for foreign R&D in China. Asia Pacific Business Review, 13(3), 425-449. doi: 10.1080/13602380701291982
Sun, Y., & Wen, K. (2007). Uncertainties, imitative behaviours and foreign R&D location: Explaining the over-concentration of foreign R&D in Beijing and Shanghai within China. Asia Pacific Business Review, 13(3), 405-424. doi: 10.1080/13602380701291966
Sun, Y., Du, D., & Huang, L. (2006). Foreign R and D in developing countries: Empirical evidence from Shanghai, China. China Review, 6(1), 67-91.
Sun, Y., Von Zedtwitz, M., & Simon, F. D. (2007). Globalization of R&D and China: An introduction. Asia Pacific Business Review, 13(3), 311-319. doi: 10.1080/13602380701291867

Sun, Y.F, D.B Du, and L Huang. 2006. "Foreign R & D in developing countries: Empirical evidence from Shanghai, China." China Review - An Interdisciplinary Journal on Greater China 6:67-91.

Sun, Yifei. 2009. "Location of foreign research and development in China." GeoJournal DOI 10.1007/s10708-009-9318-1:1-16.

Tabassum, S., Pereira, F. S., Fernandes, S., & Gama, J. (2018). Social network analysis: An overview. Wiley Interdisciplinary Reviews: Data Mining and Knowledge Discovery, 8(5), e1256.

Tang Zhihao (2011, March 17) Novartis gets stake approval. China Daily http://www.chinadaily.com.cn/business/2011-03/17/content_12185656.htm

TCS -Nokia Siemens Networks deal. (2011 April 8). Business Line. http://www.thehindubusinessline.com/todays-paper/tcs-nokia-siemens-networks-deal/article1618008.ece

Teece, D. J. 1977. "Technology Transfer by Multinational Firms: The Resource Cost of Transferring Technological Know-How." The Economic Journal 87:242-261.

Teece, D. J. 1992. "Foreign investment and technological development in Silicon Valley." California Management Review, 34:88-106.

Teece, D. J. 2005. "Technology and Technology Transfer: Mansfieldian Inspirations and Subsequent Developments." Journal of Technology Transfer 30:17-33.

The Academy for Clinical Excellence (ACE) https://www.aceindia.org/

The Internationalization of Business R&D: Evidence, Impact and implications. Paris: Organization for Ecnomic Co-Operation and Development (OECD) 2008.

The Internationalization of Corporate R&D: Leveraging the Changing Geography of Innovation. 2006 edited by

Magnus Karlsson. Östersund, Sweden: ITPS, Swedish Institute for Growth Policy Studies.

Thursby, Jerry, and Marie Thursby. 2006. "Report to the Government-Industry-Research Roundtable Here or there? A survey on the factors in multinational R&D location." Wahsington D.C.: National Academy of Sciences, National Academy of Engineering and Institute of Medicine.

Tichy, Noel M., Michael L. Tushman, and Charles Fombrun. 1979. "Social Network Analysis for Organizations." The Academy of Management Review 4:507-519.

Todo, Y., and S. Shimizutani. 2008. "Overseas R&D Activities and Home Productivity Growth: Evidence from Japanese Firm-Level Data." Journal of Industrial Economics 56:752-777.

UNCTAD, 2021, World Investment Report 2021: New York & Geneva, United Nations, 258-265 p.

UNCTAD, United Nations Conference on Trade and Development. 2005. "World Investment Report 2005: Transnational Corporations and the Internationalization of R&D." New York and Geneva, 2005: United Nations.

UNCTAD. 2001. "World investment report 2001: Promoting linkages." New York and Geneva: United Nations.

UNCTAD. 2005. "Globalization of R&D and Developing Countries: Proceedings of the Expert Meeting." Geneva: United Nations Conference on Trade and Development.

UNCTAD. 2007. "World Investment Prospect Survey 2007–2009." New York and Geneva, 2007: United Nations Conference on Trade and Development.

UNCTAD. 2009. "World Investment Report 2009: Transnational Corporations, Agricultural Production and Development." in World Investment Report 2009. New York and Geneva: United Nations.

US technology giant to share semiconductor market in China. (2005, March 07). Xinhua. Retrieved from

http://english.people.com.cn/200503/07/eng20050307_175922.html

van Bavel, R., J. Butler, P. Moncada-Paternò-Castello, A. Tübke, C. Ciupagea, V. Frigyesi, D. Gagliardi Cox, D., L. Potters, H. Hernández, J. Howells, and Y. Nugroho. 2006. "The Annual Digest of Industrial Research." Luxembourg: Offce for Offcial Publications of the European Communities.

Varsity in R&D pact with Pfizer. (2009, September 26). Business Line. Retrieved from http://www.thehindubusinessline.in/bline/2009/09/26/stories/2009092651611702.htm

Veugelers, Reinhilde and Bruno Cassiman. 2004. "Foreign subsidiaries as a channel of international technology diffusion: Some direct firm level evidence from Belgium." European Economic Review 48:455–476.

Vijay, N. (2012, April 23). MSD India invests $150 mn for R&D centre at Jamia Millia Islamic Univ, to focus on vaccines, novel molecules. http://pharmabiz.com/NewsDetails.aspx?aid=68611&sid=1

von Zedtwitz, M., and O. Gassmann. 2002. "Market versus technology drive in R&D internationalization: four different patterns of managing research and development." Research Policy 31:569-588.

Von Zedtwitz, M., Ikeda, T., Gong, L., Carpenter, R., & Hämäläinen, S. (2007). Managing foreign R&D in China. Research Technology Management, 50(3), 19-27.

von Zedtwitz, M., Ikeda, T., Gong, L., Carpenter, R., & Hämäläinen, S. (2018). Managing Foreign R&D in China: Managers of international R&D and innovation in China relate the lessons they have learned—what works and what doesn't. Research Technology Management, 61(3), 29-37.

von Zedtwitz, Maximilian, and Oliver Gassmann. 2002. "Market versus technology drive in R&D

internationalization: four different patterns of managing research and development." Research Policy 31:569–588.

von Zedtwitz, Maximilian. 2004. "Managing foreign R&D laboratories in China." R&D Management 34:439-452.

Walcott, Susan M, and James Heitzman. 2006. "High Technology Clusters in India and China: Divergent Paths." in Indian Journal of Economics and Business, edited by Penelope B. Prime and Kishore G. Kulkarni. New Delhi: Serials Publications.

Walsh, K. 2003. "Foreign High-Tech R&D in China Risks, Rewards, and Implications for U.S.-China Relations." Washington, DC: The Henry L. Stimson Center.

Walsh, K.A. 2007. "China R&D: A high-tech field of dreams." Asia Pacific Business Review 13:321-335.

Walsh, Kathleen. 2003. Foreign High-Tech R&D in China: Risks, Rewards, and Implications for U.S. China Relations. Washington: The Henry L. Stimson Center

Wang Hongyi (2011, May 17) Sanofi-Aventis redoubles efforts in Chinese market. China Daily https://www.chinadaily.com.cn/bizchina/2011-05/17/content_12525097.htm

Wen, K., & Lin, Z. (2005). The Strategic Evolution of Foreign R&D Investment in China. Paper presented at the IEEE International Engineering Management Conference.

Wen, Ke, and Zefu Lin. 2005. "The strategic evolution of foreign R&D investment in China." Engineering Management Conference, 2005. Proceedings. 2005 IEEE International.

Westney, Eleanor D. 1997. "Managing R&D in a Globalizing Economy: New Challenges." Pp. 88-106 in Technosecurity in an age of globalization: perspectives from the Pacific Rim, edited by Denis Fred Simon. New York: East Gate Book.

Xie, F. (2006). The impact of foreign R&D investment on the regional innovation systems in China: The case of

Shanghai. Paper presented at the Portland International Conference on Management of Engineering and Technology.

Xue, Lan, and Zheng Liang. 2005. "Multinational R&D in China: Myth and Realities."

Yan Y (2003 November 06) Pfizer plans clinical trial centre. China Daily http://www.chinadaily.com.cn/en/cd/2003-11/06/content_278862.htm

Yang, C. H., Matsuura, T., & Ito, T. (2019). R&D and patenting activities of foreign firms in China: The case of Japan. Japan and the World Economy, 49, 151-160. doi: 10.1016/j.japwor.2018.11.001

Zander, Ivo, and Örjan Sölvell. 2000. "Cross-Border Innovation in the Multinational Corporation: A Research Agend." International Studies of Management and Organization 30:44-67.

Zander, Ivo. 1999. "How do you mean 'global'? An empirical investigation of innovation networks in the multinational corporation." Research Policy 28:195-213.

Zanfei, Antonello. 2000. "Transnational firms and the changing organisation of innovative activities." Cambridge Journal of Economics 24:515-542.

Zedillo, E. (Ed.). 2008. The future of globalization: explorations in light of recent turbulences. New York: Routledge.

Zedtwitz, Maximilian von, Oliver Gassmann, and Roman Boutellier. 2004. "Organizing global R&D: challenges and dilemmas." Journal of International Management 10:21– 49.

Zhou W., (2020, April 8) Global pharma giants step up alliances in Chinese market. China Daily https://www.chinadaily.com.cn/a/202104/08/WS606e6066a31024ad0bab4275.html

Zhou W., (2020, November 8) Pharmaceutical companies sign deals with China's tech giants, China Daily https://www.chinadaily.com.cn/a/202011/08/WS5fa7b230a31024ad0ba83cf7.html

Zhou Wenting (2021, April 8) Global pharma giants step up alliances in Chinese market. https://www.chinadaily.com.cn/a/202104/08/WS606e6066a31024ad0bab4275.html

Zhou, W., (2021, April 15) Sanofi setting up its 1st research institute in China, China Daily https://global.chinadaily.com.cn/a/202104/15/WS60780aeca31024ad0bab5d4f.html

Zhou, Yu, and Tong Xin. 2003. "An Innovative Region in China: Interaction between Multinational Corporations and Local Firms in a High-Tech Cluster in Beijing." Economic Geography 79:129-152.

INDEX

A

AstraZeneca · xv, 91, 93, 94, 97, 112, 113, 114, 115, 116, 123, 124, 125, 126, 128, 135, 160, 167, 175, 181, 183

B

Bangalore · 54, 73, 100, 106, 132, 135, 138, 144, 147, 188
Beijing · 62, 63, 65, 77, 78, 80, 83, 102, 120, 122, 133, 136, 144, 145, 211, 217
Bristol Myers Squibb · xv, 91, 93, 94, 98, 112, 113, 115, 116, 124, 125, 126, 127, 160, 167, 176, 181

C

China · viii, ix, xi, xii, xiii, xv, xvi, 2, 3, 9, 11, 12, 13, 14, 15, 20, 23, 28, 31, 35, 38, 39, 51, 53, 55, 58, 59, 60, 61, 62, 63, 64, 65, 66, 67, 70, 74, 77, 78, 79, 80, 81, 82, 83, 84, 85, 90, 92, 93, 94, 95, 96, 98, 99, 100, 101, 102, 106, 110, 111, 112, 114, 115, 116, 117, 120, 121, 123, 125, 126, 127, 128, 130, 131, 132, 133, 134, 136, 137, 138, 141, 142, 143, 144, 145, 146, 147, 148, 149, 150, 151, 153, 154, 155, 159, 162, 166, 170, 171, 172, 173, 174, 175, 176, 177, 178, 179, 180, 185, 187, 188, 189, 190, 192, 193, 194, 195, 196, 197, 199, 200, 201, 203, 204, 205, 206, 207, 209, 210, 211, 212, 213, 214, 215, 216, 217
Cisco · xvi, 74, 75, 82, 84, 90, 92, 93, 94, 97, 102, 118, 120, 123, 137, 148, 157, 163, 171, 180, 189, 199, 201, 205, 207

D

Delhi · 54, 75, 118, 119, 134, 144, 183, 202, 205, 208, 215

E

Elsevier · xvi, 6, 90, 91, 111, 209, 210

F

Foreign Direct Investment (FDI) · xi, xii, 2, 3, 4, 11, 12, 15, 18, 19, 20, 24, 28, 32, 34, 37, 41, 54, 58, 61, 66, 71, 77, 79, 87, 105, 106, 107, 131, 143, 150, 154, 155, 183, 186, 190, 198, 201, 203, 208, 210

G

GlaxoSmithKline · xv, 91, 93, 94, 98, 100, 112, 113, 114, 115, 116, 123, 124, 125, 126, 128, 132, 161, 168, 177, 181
Gross Domestic Product (GDP) · 5, 150

H

Hewlett Packard Enterprise Company · xvi, 90
Hyderabad · 11, 54, 75, 100, 101, 144, 191, 196

I

IBM · 75, 117, 118, 119, 120, 121, 129, 130, 135, 136, 144, 146, 148, 149, 153, 158, 165, 173, 180, 196
ICT · ix, xi, xii, xv, 4, 14, 18, 36, 46, 50, 58, 62, 90, 91, 92, 94, 95, 96, 98, 99, 102, 117, 118, 119, 120, 121, 122, 128, 129, 130, 133, 136, 137, 138, 139, 141, 142, 155, 205
India · viii, ix, xi, xii, xiii, xv, xvi, 2, 3, 9, 11, 12, 13, 14, 15, 20, 23, 28, 31, 35, 38, 39, 51, 53, 54, 55, 56, 57, 58, 59, 64, 67, 70, 73, 74, 75, 76, 84, 85, 90, 92, 93, 94, 95, 96, 98, 99, 100, 101, 102, 106, 110, 111, 112, 113, 114, 117, 118, 119, 123, 125, 126, 128, 129, 131, 132, 134, 135, 137, 138, 141, 142, 143, 144, 145, 146, 147, 148, 149, 150, 151, 152, 153, 154, 155, 157, 158, 159, 160, 162, 163, 164, 165, 166, 167, 168, 169, 170, 171, 172, 173, 174, 175, 178, 183, 185, 186, 187, 188, 189, 191, 192, 197, 198, 199, 201, 202, 204, 205, 207, 208, 209, 210, 214, 215
Intel · xvi, 11, 54, 81, 90, 92, 93, 94, 97, 98, 100, 101, 118, 119, 120, 121, 124, 129, 130, 138, 144, 146, 148, 153, 159, 165, 174, 181, 191, 196, 197

J

Japan · 10, 20, 28, 30, 51, 70, 74, 146, 216
Johnson & Johnson · xv, 91, 93, 94, 98, 99, 112, 113, 116, 124, 128, 161, 168, 177, 181

K

Korea · 54, 147

M

Merck & Co. · xv, 91, 93, 98, 112, 113, 115, 116, 123, 124, 125, 134, 162, 169, 178, 181

Microsoft · xvi, 11, 62, 75, 77, 90, 92, 93, 94, 96, 97, 117, 118, 119, 120, 121, 124, 129, 132, 133, 135, 144, 146, 148, 149, 158, 165, 173, 180, 191, 199, 200, 207, 210
Motorola · xvi, 11, 54, 62, 76, 82, 117, 149, 153, 186, 199, 201
Multinational Enterprises (MINE) · 1, 15, 18, 59, 61, 198, 202, 205
Multinational Enterprises (MNE) · vii, xv, 1, 2, 4, 5, 7, 10, 11, 12, 15, 18, 19, 20, 23, 24, 25, 26, 27, 28, 29, 30, 31, 32, 33, 34, 35, 36, 37, 38, 39, 40, 47, 51, 52, 53, 54, 55, 56, 58, 59, 60, 61, 62, 63, 64, 65, 66, 67, 69, 70, 71, 72, 73, 75, 76, 77, 78, 80, 82, 87, 88, 89, 99, 100, 105, 106, 107, 108, 110, 111, 114, 117, 132, 134, 135, 141, 142, 143, 144, 145, 146, 147, 149, 150, 152, 153, 154, 190, 191, 193, 205

N

Nokia Corporation · xvi, 74, 90, 92, 96, 97, 122, 123, 157, 164, 172, 180
Novartis AG · xv, 91, 93, 94, 98, 114, 124, 162, 169, 178, 181
Novo Nordisk · xv, 91, 93, 94, 98, 112, 113, 115, 116, 124, 125, 126, 162, 169, 179, 181

P

Pfizer · xv, 82, 83, 91, 93, 98, 110, 112, 113, 114, 115, 116, 123, 124, 125, 126, 132, 137, 138, 162, 170, 179, 181, 184, 196, 206, 214, 216

Q

Qualcomm Technologies · xvi, 90, 92, 97, 98, 124, 159, 166, 174, 181

S

Samsung · xvi, 90, 93, 97, 98, 100, 118, 119, 120, 121, 124, 128, 129, 130, 146, 148, 160, 166, 175, 181
Shanghai · 62, 63, 64, 65, 77, 78, 80, 81, 82, 84, 102, 120, 121, 133, 136, 144, 145, 199, 211, 212, 216

U

U.S. · 5, 9, 10, 11, 26, 28, 30, 39, 54, 55, 59, 61, 67, 70, 72, 73, 75, 77, 79, 82, 83, 84, 106, 117, 133, 136, 142, 146, 195, 197, 213

W

Western Europe · 30, 70, 146
World Intellectual Property · xvi, 90, 96, 122

221

091221-100-1-60W